Noom Diet Cookbook

Effective Noom Diet Meal Plan & Recipes To Improve
Metabolism And Lose Weight

Christine Ensminger

Table of Content

INTRODUCTION

The Noom Diet is a weight loss program that has recently gained popularity. The Noom Diet is based on the concept of "mindful eating", which is a form of intuitive eating focused on being aware of the foods you are eating, the effects of those foods on your body, and making choices that will improve your overall health.

The Noom Diet is based on the theory that eating foods can either help or hurt your metabolism. The Noom Diet cookbook is designed to help you make choices that will improve your metabolism and help you lose weight. The Noom Diet cookbook includes recipes that are designed to help you boost your metabolism and lose weight.

The Noom Diet cookbook is divided into 3 sections: Breakfast, Lunch, and Dinner. All the recipes in this cookbook contain healthy ingredients such as lean protein, healthy fats, fruits, and vegetables.

The Noom Diet cookbook is a valuable resource for anyone who is looking to improve their metabolism and lose weight. If you are looking for a weight loss program that is based on sound science and that will help you lose weight, the Noom Diet is a great option.

(BREAKFAST RECIPES)

1. OPEN-FACED BROILED EGG SPINACH TOMATO SANDWICH

Prep Time: 5 Mins

Total Time: 5 Mins

Servings: 1

Ingredients

- ½ whole wheat English muffin
- ¼ cup of fresh spinach cooked and squeezed dry
- 1 slice tomato
- 1 hard-boiled egg sliced widthwise
- 1 tbsp mayonnaise (omega-3 enriched)

Instructions

1. Place a muffin half on a toaster oven pan. Add tomato and spinach on top. Slice one egg and arrange it in a spiral shape. Add a dollop of mayo and swirl it over the egg pieces. Add spice as desired.
2. Place under broiler for 2-3 minutes (watch carefully!) or until mayo is just beginning to brown.

Notes

1. For quick breakfast recipes like this one, I like to keep hardboiled eggs in the fridge.

2. BREAKFAST OMELETTE WITH SPINACH AND TOMATO

Prep Time: 5 Mins

Cook Time: 5 Mins

Total Time: 10 Mins

Servings: 1

Ingredients

- 2 tsp olive oil
- 1 large vine tomato
- 2 handfuls of fresh spinach or 2 cubes of frozen spinach (defrosted)
- 2 eggs
- a splash of milk
- 20g grated Parmesan cheese
- Sea salt and black pepper to season

Instructions

1. Fry the tomato and spinach in a frying pan with a splash of oil or butter.
2. Add salt and black pepper to the mixture of eggs, a splash of milk, and grated Parmesan.
3. Preheat the grill to high.
4. Add eggs to the pan with spinach and tomato, and then swirl the pan to coat everything. Cook on low heat until the eggs are set.
5. Place pan under a hot grill to finish cooking the omelette.

3. TROPICAL RASPBERRY SMOOTHIE

Prep Time: 10 Mins

Total Time: 10 Mins

Servings: 2

Ingredients

- 1 cup of water or milk of choice
- 1 cup of frozen raspberries
- 1 banana
- 2 tbsp lime juice
- 1 tsp coconut oil
- 1 tsp agave
- Ice

Instructions

1. Blend all ingredients until smooth in a high-powered blender. Add ice, if desired.

Notes

1. To taste, adjust the sweetness. You may need more or less sugar depending on the berries' acidity.

4. ROASTED VEGETABLE WRAP WITH FETA AND PESTO

Prep Time: 10 Mins

Cook Time: 20 Mins

Total Time: 30 Mins

Servings: 1

Ingredients

- Mixed vegetables (about 1 cup- see notes), cut into thin strips
- 1 tsp olive oil
- salt and pepper, to taste
- 1 Protein Up Carb Down wrap
- 1 tbsp prepared pesto
- 1 tbsp mayonnaise
- 1 tbsp crumbled feta cheese
- Handful of fresh baby spinach

Instructions

2. Preheat oven to 425 degrees Fahrenheit. Then add salt, pepper, and olive oil to the veggies (see note) on a small sheet pan. After roasting for 10 minutes, toss, then roast for an additional 10 minutes, or until browned and tender.
3. In the meantime, combine the pesto and mayonnaise in a small bowl. Leave a 1-inch margin all the way around the sides of the Protein Up Carb Down wrap before spreading the mixture evenly.
4. Place roasted veggies in the center of the wrap and add feta and spinach on top. Wrap up firmly. Enjoy right now.

Notes

1. I used carrots, red onion, portobello mushrooms, red bell peppers, zucchini, and asparagus. It will take around 20 minutes to roast carrots (or any other root vegetable or squash) (make sure to cut them small). Additionally, I enjoy roasting onions for around 20 minutes. Add softer veggies (such as asparagus, zucchini, or mushrooms) midway through the cooking process because they only need around 10 minutes to cook.
2. The instructions for roasting stay the same if you decide to roast additional veggies. You might need to extend cooking time if the pan is crowded.

5. TASTY TURKEY CHILLI

Prep Time: 5 Mins

Cook Time: 20 Mins

Total Time: 25 Mins

Servings: 2

Ingredients

- 100g turkey mince
- ½ thinly chopped white onion
- 500g passata
- Half a can of kidney beans, drained
- 1 crushed garlic clove
- 1 chopped chilli
- 1 cube of vegetable stock
- Splash of water
- ½ tsp paprika
- ½ tsp oregano
- ½ tsp cayenne pepper
- ½ tsp cumin

Instructions

1. Cook the turkey mince till brown in a skillet, then drain any extra fat.
2. Add the onion and sauté until soft. Combine all the ingredients, excluding the water, and adjust the sauce's thickness as needed.
3. Add pepper and salt to taste.
4. Add cheese if desired and serve with rice or potato wedges!

6. HONEY GARLIC LIME GLAZED SHRIMP

Prep Time: 5 Mins

Cook Time: 5 Mins

Total Time: 10 Mins

Servings: 2

Ingredients

- 1 cup of raw or cooked shrimp
- 2 tbsp soy sauce
- 3 tbsp honey
- 3 minced garlic cloves
- green onions for garnish
- 2 limes juiced

Instructions

1. Add all ingredients (excluding shrimp) to a small saucepan and simmer on low for seven minutes, stirring occasionally.
2. Add the shrimp and cook for 2 more minutes, flipping once (If using cooked shrimp, coat it with the sauce and boil for a minute.)
3. Add some green onions to your shrimp as a garnish.
4. Enjoy it without rice or as is!

7. CHIA, HEMP HEARTS & YOGURT BREAKFAST

Prep Time: 2 Mins

Total Time: 2 Mins

Servings: 1

Ingredients

- 1 cup of Greek yogurt
- 1 tbsp chia seeds
- 1 tbsp hemp hearts
- 1 Ounce raspberries (No need to measure an exact ounce with a handful of raspberries)
- 1 Ounce blackberries
- 1 Ounce walnuts

Instructions

1. Add yogurt to the breakfast bowl.
2. Add berries, walnuts, hemp hearts, and chia seeds last.
3. Mix it up and enjoy. Add extra honey or vanilla Greek yogurt to the dish if you like the flavor to be a little sweeter. Your flavor will be sweeter with any choice. Alternately, include softened bananas into the mixture, which tend to enhance the flavor.

8. MATCHA CHIA PUDDING

Prep Time: 5 Mins

Total Time: 5 Mins

Servings: 1

Ingredients

- ¼ cup of chia seeds
- 1½ cups of non-dairy milk or water (or a combination)
- 2 tsp matcha green tea powder
- ½ tbsp maple syrup, or 3–4 drops pure stevia extract
- ½ tsp vanilla extract
- Optional toppings: fruit, granola, seeds, nuts

Instructions

1. Put the chia seeds, non-dairy milk, and a medium bowl together. Combined by stirring.
2. Add matcha powder to a small bowl. Add some hot water and whisk until smooth. (By doing this, the matcha powder won't clump when combined with the chia pudding.)
3. Stir in the matcha mixture, vanilla, maple syrup, and chia seeds. Put it in the refrigerator and let it there for a minimum of two to three hours.
4. Add fresh fruit, granola, and other garnishes on top.

9. APPLE CINNAMON OATMEAL PORRIDGE

Prep Time: 5 Mins

Cook Time: 15 Mins

Total Time: 20 Mins

Servings: 2

Ingredients

Oatmeal

- 1 cup of thick-cut Rolled oats
- 1 medium peeled & diced Granny smith apple
- 4 cups of Almond milk (You can use your fave plant-based milk!)
- ½ cup of condensed milk
- ¼ cup of pure maple syrup
- 1 tbsp ground cinnamon
- 1 tsp ground nutmeg
- ½ tsp ground allspice
- Pinch of sea salt

Caramelized apples

- 1 medium Gala apples, sliced with skin on
- 2 tbsp unsalted butter
- 1 tsp ground cinnamon
- ½ cup of organic brown sugar
- pinch of sea salt

Topping

- Toasted walnuts or pecans (See Notes!)

Instructions

To make oatmeal

1. Stir the oats, apple cubes, milk, cinnamon, allspice, nutmeg, and sea salt in a medium pot over medium heat until everything is mixed. Put everything in a pot and boil, then turn the heat down so that it simmers for 8-10 minutes while you stir it occasionally.
2. When done, oats should be thick, swelled, fluffy, and creamy with half the liquid left. Stir in the condensed milk and maple syrup and continue to cook for another 1-2 minutes before removing from the heat.

Caramelized apples

3. Add the butter to a medium pan and cook until it melts over medium-high heat. Stir for about 2-3 minutes, or until the brown sugar, cinnamon, and sea salt are mixed and the mixture starts to boil.
4. Add the apple slices, mix to combine, and simmer for 8 to 10 minutes, till the apples are soft and the sauce has thickened. Get rid of the heat.
5. Pour oatmeal into serving bowl(s) and top with toasted nuts, caramelized apples, and optionally, a light drizzle of maple syrup.

Notes

1. **Storage:** Refrigerate for up to 5 days. Ideal for week's worth of meal preparation!
2. **Overnight option:** Simply combine all of the ingredients for the oatmeal in a bowl. Refrigerate overnight with a tight-fitting plastic wrap over the bowl (or at least 8 hours). When ready to serve, top overnight oats with caramelized apples.
3. **Toasted nuts:** Place chopped walnuts and/or pecans on a baking sheet, stirring them halfway through toasting at 400 degrees Fahrenheit for 5-10 minutes to prevent browning on one side.
4. **Sweetener:** You can simply add Agave to oatmeal as a sweetener in place of maple syrup.
5. **Vegan option:** Substitute canned full-fat coconut milk or cream for the condensed milk, and replace the unsalted butter with vegan butter.

10. EASY OVERNIGHT OATS

Prep Time: 8 Mins

Total Time: 8 Mins

Servings: 1

Ingredients

Basic Overnight Oats

- ½ cup of old fashioned rolled oats
- ½ cup of milk, any milk will work
- ¼ cup of plain yogurt or ¼ cup of more milk
- 1-2 tsp maple syrup or honey
- 1 tsp chia seeds (optional)
- ½ tsp vanilla extract (optional)
- pinch of sea salt
- toppings of choice: fruit nut butter, seeds,nuts, etc.

Chocolate Chip Overnight Oats

- 2 tbsp chocolate chips

Peanut Butter Overnight Oats

- 1 tbsp peanut butter

Berry Overnight Oats

- ¼ cup of fresh berries

Instructions

Basic Overnight Oats

1. Add oats, milk, maple syrup, yogurt, chia seeds, vanilla, and sea salt to a sealed jar or storage container. Combine ingredients by stirring. Place overnight in the refrigerator. You can reduce the soak period to 2-4 hours if you're in a hurry.
2. Remove lid the next morning (or whenever you're ready to eat) and thoroughly mix the oats. You may add a bit more milk to the mixture to thin them down if they look too thick. Add your preferred toppings and indulge. The oats can be consumed directly from the jar or put into a dish to be served.

3. Store overnight oats can be in the fridge for maximum 5 days in an airtight container.

Chocolate Chip Overnight Oats

4. Stir 1 tbsp of chocolate chips into the overnight oat mixture during preparation, then sprinkle the remaining chocolate chips over the oats before serving.

Peanut Butter Overnight Oats

5. Mix ½ tsp of peanut butter into the overnight oat mixture during preparation, then sprinkle remaining peanut butter over the oats before serving.

Berry Overnight Oats

6. Mix 2 tbsp of berries into the oat mixture the night before, and then serve with the rest of the berries on top.

11. QUINOA PORRIDGE RECIPE

Prep Time: 5 Mins

Total Time: 5 Mins

Servings: 2

Ingredients

- 1 cup of cooked quinoa
- 1 and ½ cups of almond milk or your favorite milk
- ½ tsp pure vanilla extract
- 1 tsp maple syrup

Toppings

- fresh fruit
- nuts
- seeds
- peanut or almond butter

Instructions

1. To prepare quinoa porridge, mix approximately half cup of quinoa with 1 cup of milk or less.
2. Add vanilla essence for flavor and maple syrup or another sweetener of your choice for sweetness. Serve garnished with fresh fruit, seeds, and nuts.

Notes

To cook quinoa

1. The general guideline is that 1 cup of quinoa requires 1.5 cups of water. This results in a 1:1.5 ratio and 3 cups of cooked quinoa (about 6 portions).
2. Bring water and washed quinoa to a boil in a saucepan. Now put the lid on and turn the heat down to minimum when the water boils; cook it covered for 15 minutes.
3. Remove from the heat, cover it, and allow it to cool for five more minutes. Remove the lid lastly, then fluff with a fork!

12. FRUIT DELIGHT

Prep Time: 5 Mins

Total Time: 5 Mins

Servings: 1

Ingredients

- 1 toasted English Muffin
- 3 sliced strawberries
- ½ peach diced
- butter
- 1 tsp cinnamon

Instructions

1. Spread butter on an English muffin.
2. Sprinkle cinnamon on top of the English muffins.
3. Add strawberries and peaches on top.
4. Enjoy.

13. HEALTHY OATMEAL BLUEBERRY PANCAKES

Prep Time: 3 Mins

Cook Time: 7 Mins

Total Time: 10 Mins

Servings: 1

Ingredients

- ½ cup of oats
- 2 tbsp yogurt
- ⅓ tsp baking soda
- ⅓ tsp baking powder
- 1 tsp vanilla
- 1 egg
- ⅓ cup of blueberries
- 1 tbsp maple syrup
- Coconut oil for the pan

Instructions

1. Whisk all the ingredients (apart from the blueberries) in a blender until completely smooth. If you're using ground oats, you may also use a hand blender and a bowl, or simply a bowl and a fork.
2. Grease a nonstick skillet with coconut oil over medium heat and pour the pancake batter, forming smaller-sized pancakes (the size of your palm, this will make flipping easier). Add blueberries to the uncooked side.
3. When the edges seem done and bubbles appear, use the spatula to work your way around the edges of the pancakes and flip the pancakes. Continue until the batter runs out.
4. Serve right away with more blueberries and some maple syrup or honey.

14. BABY SPINACH OMELET

Prep Time: 5 Mins

Cook Time: 10 Mins

Total Time: 15 Mins

Servings: 1

Ingredients

- 2 eggs
- 1 cup of torn baby spinach leaves
- 1 ½ tbsp grated Parmesan cheese
- ¼ tsp onion powder
- ⅛ tsp ground nutmeg
- salt and pepper to taste

Directions

1. Scramble some eggs, then fold in some baby spinach and some Parmesan. Add nutmeg, onion powder, salt, and pepper for flavoring.
2. Spray cooking spray in a small skillet and heat it up. Add the egg mixture after it's heated, and simmer for 3 minutes or until it's half set. Cook for another 2-3 minutes after flipping using a spatula.
3. Decrease the heat to low and cook the omelet for another 2-3 minutes, or until it is done to your liking.

15. AVOCADO TOAST

Prep Time: 3 Mins

Cook Time: 2 Mins

Total Time: 5 Mins

Servings: 1

Ingredients

- 1 slice of bread
- ½ ripe avocado
- Pinch of salt

Instructions

1. Toast your bread till brown and firm.
2. Take off the pit of your avocado. Scoop out the meat using a large spoon. Put it in a bowl and mash it with a fork until it is as smooth as you like. Add a small amount of salt (about ⅛ tsp) and taste before adding more, if desired.
3. Spread avocado on top of your bread. Enjoy as-is or top with any (If you have some flaky sea salt handy, I highly suggest adding a light sprinkle).

16. EGG AND TOMATO SCRAMBLE

Total Time: 15 Mins

Servings: 1

Ingredients

- 1 plum peeled and chopped tomato
- 1 tsp chopped fresh basil or ¼ tsp dried basil
- 1 egg or egg substitute equivalent
- 1 tsp water
- 1 minced garlic clove
- 1 tsp olive oil, optional
- Salt and pepper to taste, optional
- 1 slice bread, toasted
- Additional fresh basil, optional

Directions

1. Mix tomato and basil in a small bowl; leave aside. Whisk the egg, water, and garlic in a separate bowl. Warm oil in a small nonstick pan; add egg mixture. Gently cook and whisk the egg until it almost sets. Add the tomato mixture along as any additional seasonings.
2. Cook and stir tomato and egg until both are well cooked. Serve with toast. If desired, garnish with basil.

17. STRAWBERRY MANGO SMOOTHIE

Prep Time: 5 Mins

Cook Time: 1 Mins

Total Time: 6 Mins

Servings: 1

Ingredients

- 1 cup of spinach
- 1 cup of almond milk
- 1 cup of strawberries frozen
- ½ cup of mango frozen
- 1 serving Protein Smoothie Boost (optional)

Instructions

1. **Blend:** spinach and almond milk in blender.
2. **Add:** remaining fruit and blend again.

Notes

1. To make the smoothie chilly or serve it with ice, use at least one frozen fruit.

18. GRILLED BANANA SANDWICHES RECIPE

Prep Time: 5 Mins

Cook Time: 10 Mins

Total Time: 15 Mins

Servings: 2

Ingredients

- 1½ tbsp whipped cream cheese low-fat
- 1½ tbsp peanut butter
- 1 tbsp honey
- 1 pinch salt
- 4 slices whole-grain bread

Instructions

1. Slice a banana in half, then mash with a fork in a bowl. Add salt, honey, peanut butter, and cream cheese.
2. Spread onto 2 pieces of bread
3. Place a sizable skillet over medium-high heat after spraying it with cooking spray. Cut the last banana in half crosswise, then in half lengthwise.
4. Cook the banana halves until they are caramelized in a pan.
5. Then, cover the remaining bread with the bananas and cream cheese.
6. Clean the skillet, then place it over medium heat with a spritz of additional cooking spray. Add the sandwiches and heat them until both sides are browned.

Notes

1. The recipe for a fried banana sandwich from Noom is a delicious treat that is yet rather healthy. Fun at any time of day, including for breakfast.

19. RASPBERRY LIME SMOOTHIE FROM NOOM

Prep Time: 3 Mins

Cook Time: 2 Mins

Total Time: 5 Mins

Servings: 2

Ingredients

- 2 cups of hulled raspberries, blueberries, or strawberries
- 1 banana
- ½ cup of orange juice
- 1 tbsp lime
- ½ cup of crushed ice
- 2 mint leaves or lime wedges garnish

Instructions

1. Combine all the ingredients in a blender (except garnish) and blund until smooth.
2. Pour into 2 glasses and garnish with mint leaves or lime wedge.

Notes

1. This smoothie recipe for breakfast is quick and nutritious. There's no need to make things complicated; simply store these items in your fruit bowl, refrigerator, and freezer.

20. HEALTHY BREAKFAST BURRITO RECIPE

Prep Time: 8 Mins

Cook Time: 7 Mins

Total Time: 15 Mins

Servings: 1

Ingredients

- 2 eggs
- 1 jalapeno, slices
- 1 tbsp cream cheese
- 1 tbsp tomato paste
- 1 garlic clove (optional)
- ⅓ cup of washed spinach
- ¼ large avocado
- 1 thinly sliced scallion
- 2 heaping tbsp mozzarella cheese
- 2 tsp olive oil
- Sausage (optional)
- tortilla, large

Instructions

1. Put the eggs in a nonstick skillet and softly scramble them.
2. To make a creamy spread, combine the cream cheese, tomato paste, 1 tsp of olive oil, and optional garlic. Cover the tortilla with this. Cook a sausage as well, if preferred. Clean the pan before toasting the tortilla.
3. All remaining ingredients, excluding olive oil, should be added to the tortilla before the burrito is wrapped.
4. Toast the folded side first over medium high heat with olive oil to seal the ends. Do this until it turns golden, then flip it over and toast the other side as well.
5. Transfer to a chopping board, then carefully slice through the center. Serve right away!

21. CUSTOMIZABLE MICROWAVE EGGS (GF, LOW CAL, PALEO)

Cook Time: 2 Mins

Total Time: 2 Mins

Servings: 1

Ingredients

Base Recipe

- 2 eggs or 4 egg whites for higher protein
- 2 tbsp unsweetened almond milk
- salt and pepper to taste

Optional Add In's

- ⅛ cup of broccoli rice
- ½ tsp garlic powder
- ½ tsp thyme

Instructions

1. Spray a 12-15 ouncecup (or cereal dish) with olive oil spray.
2. Add milk, pepper, salt, and eggs. Combine ingredients and whisk until eggs are frothy and yolks are split up. Add more add-ins or optional ones as needed. To blend, stir.
3. After that, place the cup in the microwave for 30 seconds at a time, stirring and checking after each interval.
4. Eggs are usually done cooking after 1:30 or 2:00 minutes.
5. Remove from the microwave and serve (or take with you on the go)!

22. SCRAMBLED EGGS AND CHEESE

Prep Time: 10 Mins

Total Time: 10 Mins

Servings: 1

Ingredients

- 2 large eggs
- 2 tbsp milk
- ⅛ tsp cayenne pepper
- ¼ tsp salt
- 1 thinly sliced scallion
- 2 tbsp shredded cheddar cheese
- 1 grape or cherry tomato, quartered lengthwise

Directions

1. Combine the eggs, milk, cayenne pepper, and salt in a large (10-ounce), microwave-safe custard cup or ramekin. Add scallion and stir.
2. Microwave (uncovered) for 45 seconds; mix with a fork. Cook the eggs for another 45 seconds or so, or until they are almost set. Take out of the microwave.
3. Add the shredded cheddar cheese and toss with a clean fork before covering with a paper towel or a clean kitchen towel. Let rest for approximately a minute, or until eggs are set and cheese has melted. Add a cherry or grape tomato on top, then serve right away.

23. APPLE BANANA NUT OATMEAL

Prep Time: 2 Mins

Cook Time: 5 Mins

Total Time: 7 Mins

Servings: 1

Ingredients

- 1 cup of skim milk
- 1 cup of water
- 1 tsp vanilla
- 1 tsp cinnamon
- ¼ tsp nutmeg
- 1 pinch sea salt
- 1 cup of old-fashioned oats
- 1 sliced banana
- 1 diced apple
- 2 tbsp flax seed meal
- 2 tbsp chopped walnuts

Instructions

1. Mix the following ingredients in a pot over medium heat: milk, water, vanilla, cinnamon, nutmeg, and a dash of salt.
2. Add oats, banana, and apple after gradually bringing to a boil.
3. Decrease heat to low and simmer for 5 minutes after boiling the mixture.
4. Stir regularly and finish with the flax and walnuts.
5. Serve oatmeal when the required consistency is obtained.

24. SCRAMBLED EGGS WITH BASIL, SPINACH & TOMATOES

Prep Time: 5 Mins

Cook Time: 5 Mins

Total Time: 10 Mins

Servings: 2

Ingredients

- 1 tbsp olive oil, plus 1 tsp
- 3 halved tomatoes
- 4 large eggs
- 4 tbsp natural bio yogurt
- ⅓ small pack chopped basil
- 175 grams of well-dried baby spinach (if it needs washing)

Instructions

1. Warm 1 tsp of oil in a large, non-stick frying pan. Add the tomatoes, cut-side down, and cook over medium heat. Add the eggs and beat with the yogurt, 2 tbsp of water, a good amount of black pepper, and the basil in a jug while the potatoes are boiling.
2. Place the tomatoes on serving platters. Add spinach to the pan and wilt it with a few stirs while the eggs cook.
3. Scramble the eggs with the remaining oil in a nonstick pan over medium heat, stirring occasionally, until the eggs are just set. Place a serving of spinach on each plate, then top with scrambled eggs.

25. AVOCADO AND EGG LUNCH

Prep Time: 3 Mins

Cook Time: 7 Mins

Total Time: 10 Mins

Servings: 1

Ingredients

- 1 peeled avocado, sliced into 8 wedges
- 1 egg poached
- 8 stalks roasted baby asparagus
- 1 tbsp balsamic vinegar
- Black pepper fresh ground

Instructions

1. Preheat the oven to 350 degrees Fahrenheit. Place the baby asparagus on a small baking sheet. Drizzle some olive oil over the top, then shake and roll the pan to coat the asparagus stalks. Roll the stalks in a spoonful of balsamic vinegar.
2. Boil some water in a small saucepan. After that, bake the asparagus for 5-7 minutes, being careful not to overcook it. Poach the egg for around 3 minutes.
3. Peel, wedge, and arrange the avocado in a spiral on a platter while the egg is poaching and the asparagus is baking.
4. Place the poached egg in the middle of the asparagus and avocado wedges on the platter. Add freshly ground black pepper and more balsamic vinegar, if you want, as a garnish.

26. QUINOA BREAKFAST SCRAMBLE

Prep Time: 5 Mins

Cook Time: 5 Mins

Total Time: 10 Mins

Servings: 1

Ingredients

- ½ cup of cooked quinoa
- 2 scrambled eggs
- ½ cubed avocado
- 1 tbsp salsa
- ½ tsp lemon pepper
- ¼ tsp garlic salt

Instructions

1. Place the eggs and avocado on top of the quinoa in a serving bowl. Add salsa over top and finish with salt and lemon pepper.

27. TOFU SCRAMBLE

Prep Time: 10 Mins

Cook Time: 20 Mins

Total Time: 30 Mins

Servings: 2

Ingredients

- 1 tbsp olive oil
- 1 small finely sliced onion
- 1 large crushed garlic clove
- ½ tsp turmeric
- 1 tsp ground cumin
- ½ tsp sweet smoked paprika
- 280g extra firm tofu

- 100g cherry tomatoes, halved
- ½ small bunch chopped parsley
- rye bread, to serve, (optional)

Instructions

1. Warm the oil in a frying pan over medium heat and gently cook the onion for 8-10 minutes, or until golden brown and sticky. Cook for one minute after adding the garlic, paprika, turmeric, and cumin.
2. Mash the tofu in a bowl with a fork, leaving some chunks. Add to the pan, and cook for three minutes. Increase the heat, add the tomatoes, and simmer for an additional five minutes, or until they start to soften. Combine the mixture with the parsley. If you want, serve it alone or with toasted rye bread that contains gluten.

28. ZUCCHINI BREAD OATMEAL

Prep Time: 5 Mins

Cook Time: 10 Mins

Total Time: 15 Mins

Servings: 1

Ingredients

- ½ cup of old fashioned oats
- ½ sliced banana
- ¼ cup of grated zucchini
- ½ tsp cinnamon
- ½ tsp vanilla
- pinch of sea salt
- 1 cup of unsweetened almond milk or water
- ½ tbsp chopped walnuts
- 1 tbsp almond butter or another type of nut butter

Instructions

1. Add the oats, banana, zucchini, cinnamon, and sea salt to a medium pot. Stir in the almond milk and water after adding them. Boil for 8-10 minutes over medium-high heat, or until all liquid has been absorbed. Stir the oats many times while cooking to

ensure that the banana slices melt into the oats and that the oats do not adhere to the pot. When the oatmeal is finished cooking, all of the liquid will have been absorbed, and the oats will have become thick and fluffy.

2. Place some oats in a bowl, then top with almond butter and chopped walnuts!

29. AVOCADO & BLACK BEAN EGGS

Prep Time: 5 Mins

Cook Time: 5 Mins

Total Time: 10 Mins

Servings: 2

Ingredients

- 2 tsp rapeseed oil
- 1 deseeded and thinly sliced red chill
- 1 large sliced garlic clove
- 2 large eggs
- 400g can black beans
- ½ x 400g can cherry tomatoes
- ¼ tsp cumin seeds
- 1 halved and sliced small avocado
- handful fresh, chopped coriander
- 1 lime, cut into wedges

Instructions

1. Heat the oil in a big nonstick frying pan. Cook the garlic and chili until they are tender and beginning to color. Break the eggs into the pan on all sides. Spoon the beans (with liquid) and tomatoes about the pan once they begin to firm, then top with cumin seeds. You want to warm the beans and tomatoes, not boil them.
2. After turning off the heat, sprinkle the avocado and cilantro on top. Slice half of the lime wedges in half. Serve with the remaining wedges to squeeze over before eating.

30. BRUSCHETTA BURGER BOWL

Prep Time: 10 Mins

Cook Time: 5 Mins

Total Time: 15 Mins

Servings: 1

Ingredients

- 3 cups of chopped lettuce
- ½ cup of seeded and chopped tomatoes
- 2 tbsp. chopped fresh basil, or more for topping
- 1 tbsp. balsamic vinegar
- 1 ½ tsp. olive oil
- 1 tsp. chopped garlic
- ½ tsp. Italian seasoning
- 4Ounce raw extra-lean ground beef (at least 96% lean)
- ⅓ cup of chopped onion
- ⅛ tsp. each salt and black pepper
- 2 tbsp. shredded part-skim mozzarella cheese

Directions

1. Put lettuce in a big bowl.
2. Mix tomatoes, basil, vinegar, oil, garlic, and ¼ tsp. Italian spice in a medium bowl. Stir well, then spoon over the lettuce.
3. Warm a nonstick-coated skillet over medium-high heat. Add the steak, onion, remaining ¼ tsp. Italian seasoning, salt, and pepper. Now cook for about 5 minutes, or until the steak is thoroughly cooked and the onion has softened.
4. Place the meat mixture in the big bowl. Add cheese on top.

31. HEALTHY SHAKSHUKA

Prep Time: 10 Mins

Cook Time: 30 Mins

Total Time: 40 Mins

Servings: 2

Ingredients

- 1 tbsp cold pressed rapeseed oil
- 1 red onion, cut into thin wedges
- 1 finely sliced red pepper
- 1 finely sliced yellow pepper
- 3 large crushed garlic cloves
- 1 tsp cumin seeds
- 1 tsp crushed coriander seeds
- 1 heaped tsp sweet smoked paprika
- 400g can cherry tomatoes
- 115g baby spinach
- 4 medium eggs
- ½ small bunch of roughly chopped coriander
- ½ small bunch of roughly chopped dill

Instructions

1. Prepare a big, nonstick frying pan and heat the oil. Add the onion and peppers, and cook for 8-10 minutes, or until the vegetables start to soften. Add garlic, cumin, coriander, and paprika and cook for an additional minute. Add the tomatoes, spinach, and 100 ml of water, then bring to a boil until the spinach has wilted. Decrease the heat to a simmer, cover the pot, and cook for 10 minutes, according to taste.
2. Gently press an egg into the four holes you made in the tomato mixture. Cover with a cover or foil and simmer for 8-10 minutes or until the eggs are just set. Remove the lid, sprinkle the fresh herbs on top, and serve.

32. BANANA OAT PANCAKES

Prep Time: 5 Mins

Cook Time: 15 Mins

Total Time: 20 Mins

Servings: 2

Ingredients

- 125ml oat milk
- 2 egg, separated
- 1 small banana
- 100g rolled oats
- 2 tsp baking powder
- Few drops of vanilla extract
- Avocado oil spray
- low-fat yogurt and fruit to top

Instructions

1. Put the oat milk, banana, egg yolks, oats, baking powder, and vanilla extract into a blender, and pulse the mixture until it is as smooth as possible. Whisk the egg whites until firm peaks form. Add 1-2 tbsp of the egg whites to the mixture and fold in the remaining whites.
2. Cook the batter for approximately 1-2 minutes, or until the base is firm and bubbles emerge all over the top, in a nonstick pan heated over medium heat and sprayed with a whisper of oil. Cook for a minute on the opposite side. Repeat in batches, ensuring that the top appears to be drying out a bit before attempting the flip, or the center will collapse.

33. FARMERS MARKET BREAKFAST BOWLS

Prep Time: 20 Mins

Cook Time: 10 Mins

Total Time: 30 Mins

Servings: 2

Ingredients

Spiced "Riced" Carrots

- 2 medium carrots
- 2 tsp lemon juice
- 1 tsp extra-virgin olive oil
- ¼ tsp cumin
- ¼ tsp coriander
- sea salt and freshly ground black pepper

Yogurt Green Goddess Sauce (makes extra)

- 2 cups of whole milk Greek yogurt
- 2 tbsp lemon juice
- 2 tbsp extra-virgin olive oil
- 2 garlic cloves
- ½ tsp sea salt
- ⅓ cup of chives, reserve some for garnish
- ⅓ cup of fresh basil
- ¼ cup of fresh mint
- Freshly ground black pepper

For the bowls

- handful of salad greens
- 1 medium shredded or very finely diced beet
- 4 thinly sliced radishes
- 2 small tomatoes, sliced into wedges
- 2 soft boiled eggs (see notes)
- extra-virgin olive oil, for drizzling
- sea salt and freshly ground black pepper

Instructions

Make the spiced carrot salad

1. Grate the carrots (easiest using the grating plate in a food processor). Put the carrots in a small bowl and add salt, pepper, cumin, coriander, lemon juice, and olive oil to taste. Set your food processor aside and clean it.

Make the yogurt green goddess sauce

2. Blend the yogurt, lemon juice, olive oil, garlic, and salt in the food Processor until well-combined. Add the chives, basil, and mint and pulse until mixed.
3. Put salad greens, carrots, radishes, tomatoes, shredded beet, and soft-boiled eggs in the bowls. Sprinkle salt and pepper over the bowls after adding a drizzle of olive oil. Dollop some yogurt sauce on top before serving.
4. Chill yogurt sauce for three to four days. Use it as a dip for veggies, slather it on sandwiches, or drizzle it over salads.

Notes

1. To make soft-boiled eggs: Put water to boil in a medium pot, then reduce heat to maintain a slow simmer. Carefully drop the eggs into water with a slotted spoon, and then simmer for 7 minutes. Remove and quickly cool for about 3 minutes in a dish of cold water. When the eggs are completely cold, tap each one on the bottom to slightly fracture the shell. Carefully slide a small spoon in and around the egg to loosen it and get it out of the shell. Separate the peeled eggs.

34. POACHED EGGS WITH SMASHED AVOCADO & TOMATOES

Prep Time: 10 Mins

Total Time: 10 Mins

Servings: 2

Ingredients

- 2 tomatoes, halved
- ½ tsp rapeseed oil
- 2 eggs
- 1 small ripe avocado
- 2 slices seeded wholemeal soda bread
- 2 handfuls rocket

Instructions

1. Warm a nonstick frying pan, spray the cut surface of the tomatoes liberally with oil, and cook them in the pan, cut side down until softened and slightly caramelized. Poach eggs in a pan of boiling water for approximately 1-2 minutes, or until the whites are set but yolks are still runny.
2. After that, slice the avocado in half, remove the stone, then scoop out the meat and spread it over the toast. Add the eggs, some freshly ground black pepper, and a few rocket pieces to each serving. Serve the tomatoes separately.

35. CINNAMON QUINOA BREAKFAST BOWL

Prep Time: 5 Mins

Cook Time: 20 Mins

Total Time: 25 Mins

Servings: 2

Ingredients

- ½ cup of uncooked quinoa
- 1 cup of Almond Breeze Almond milk, Original or Vanilla
- 1-2 cinnamon sticks
- piece of a vanilla bean, or ½ tsp pure vanilla extract
- pinch of salt

Toppings

- toasted sliced almonds
- toasted coconut flakes
- peaches
- raspberries
- maple syrup, optional
- extra splashes of almond milk, optional
- more spices, to taste (cinnamon, nutmeg, etc.), optional

Instructions

1. Drain and rinse the quinoa.
2. Add the almond milk, vanilla, salt, and up to two cinnamon sticks to it in a small pot. Cook for 15 minutes on a medium heat after raising to a high heat. (Tip: Don't just walk away; if it begins boiling, turn off the heat, give it a stir if necessary, and then continue.)
3. Remove the skillet from the heat after 15 minutes, then let the quinoa rest for another 5 minutes to allow the almond milk to be absorbed and the quinoa to finish cooking. Taste and adjust the spices to your preference.
4. Top the quinoa with fruit, toasted coconut, and almonds after scooping it into two dishes. Alternatively, serve with maple syrup. Take pleasure in as a fluffy pilaf or more as a porridge with warm almond milk drizzled on top.

Notes

1. Quinoa may be kept in the fridge for 4-5 days after cooking. Heat it just before serving or serve it at room temperature. Add a couple extra dashes of almond milk if it's too dry.
2. You may use whatever seasonal fruit you desire for this; dried fruits are also great.

36. BAKED FALAFEL BOWL

Prep Time: 8 Hrs 10 Mins

Cook Time: 20 Mins

Total Time: 30 Mins

Ingredients

- 10 baked falafel
- 1 cup of Mediterranean roasted cauliflower
- 1 roasted red pepper
- 1 cup of cabbage mix
- ¼ cup of sliced cucumber
- ¼ cup of diced tomato
- ¼ cup of diced red onion
- 2 tbsp lemon juice
- 1 pinch sea salt
- ¼ cup of feta
- 1 avocado
- ¼ cup of tahini
- ¼ cup of hummus

Instructions

1. Place the frozen falafel in a 350°F preheated oven for 20-30 minutes, flipping once halfway through.
2. Bake the red pepper for 15 minutes at 350°F after mixing with 1 tbsp of olive oil and salt.
3. Add salt, lemon juice, and chopped tomatoes to a bowl.
4. Put the cabbage mixture in a big dish and serve. Top with cucumber, roasted cauliflower, roasted red pepper, sliced avocado, feta, baked falafel, onion-tomato combination, and baked falafel. Serve after tahini drizzling!

37. BAKED EGGS WITH TOMATOES AND FETA CHEESE

Prep Time: 5 Mins

Cook Time: 15 Mins

Total Time: 20 Mins

Servings: 2

Ingredients

- ½ cup of chopped Beefsteak tomato
- ½ cup of crumbled Feta Cheese of good quality
- 4 eggs
- ¼ tsp dried oregano
- Olive Oil Spray

Instructions

1. Set the oven to 375 degrees Fahrenheit.
2. Spray some olive oil on the ramekins;
3. Add ¼ cup each to each ramekin of chopped tomatoes and crumbled feta.
4. Add 2 eggs to each ramekin and garnish with dry oregano.
5. Add some freshly ground pepper and salt;
6. Place it in the hot oven and cook for 15–17 minutes or longer if the egg whites are still flowing. Keep an eye on it so the yolks don't become overdone.

38. EGG NIÇOISE SALAD

Prep Time: 10 Mins

Cook Time: 10 Mins

Total Time: 20 Mins

Servings: 2

Ingredients

For the dressing

- 2 tbsp rapeseed oil
- juice 1 lemon
- 1 tsp balsamic vinegar
- 1 grated garlic clove
- ⅓ small pack chopped basil, leaves
- 3 pitted rinsed and chopped black Kalamata olive

For the salad

- 2 eggs
- 250g thickly sliced new potatoes
- 200g fine green beans
- ½ very finely chopped red onion
- 14 halved cherry tomatoes
- 6 leaves of romaine lettuce, torn into bite-sized pieces
- 6 pitted rinsed and halved black Kalamata olive

Instructions

1. Combine dressing ingredients in a small dish with 1 tbsp of water.
2. While this is going on, boil the potatoes for 7 minutes. Then add the beans and simmer for an additional 5 minutes, or until both are just soft. Boil two eggs for eight minutes, then shell and cut in half.
3. Combine the beans, potatoes, and remaining salad ingredients (except the eggs) in a large bowl with half of dressing. Sprinkle the remaining dressing over the top after placing the eggs.

39. CUCUMBER SANDWICH

Prep Time: 10 Mins

Total Time: 10 Mins

Servings: 1

Ingredients

- 2 ounces cream cheese, at room temperature
- 1 tbsp low-fat plain Greek yogurt
- 1 tbsp sliced fresh chives
- 1 tbsp chopped fresh dill
- ¼ tsp ground pepper
- 2 slices whole-wheat sandwich bread
- ⅓ cup of thinly sliced English cucumber

Directions

1. Stir together cream cheese, yogurt, chives, dill, and pepper in a small bowl until thoroughly combined. Evenly distribute the mixture on one side of each bread piece. Place sliced cucumber on one slice of bread before covering it with the second slice, cream cheese side up. Remove the sandwich's crusts and halve it diagonally.

40. BLT PASTA SALAD

Prep Time: 10 Mins

Cook Time: 10 Mins

Total Time: 20 Mins

Servings: 1

Ingredients

- 25g pasta bows
- 2 cooked rashers of crispy bacon, chopped
- 15g chopped spinach
- 6 halved cherry tomatoes
- ½ tbsp crème fraîche
- ¼ tsp wholegrain mustard

Instructions

1. Cook the pasta according to package directions the night before school, then run it under cold water to cool fast. Add the crème fraîche, bacon, mustard, spinach, and tomatoes, and season with a little salt. Spoon into a jar that can close tightly, then refrigerate overnight.

41. STOVETOP TURMERIC OATMEAL

Prep Time: 5 Mins

Cook Time: 5 Mins

Total Time: 10 Mins

Servings: 2

Ingredients

- 1 mashed banana
- 1.5cups of oats
- 2 cups of milk of choice
- ¾ tsp ground turmeric
- ¼ salt
- ¼ tsp ground ginger
- ¼ tsp cinnamon
- 1 tbsp maple syrup
- 1 tbsp chia seeds
- pinch of black pepper, optional (see notes)

Instructions

1. Put banana in a bowl and mash it with a fork.
2. Combine your oats, milk, turmeric, salt, ginger, cinnamon, and maple syrup in a small or medium pot.
3. Cook the oats in a pot of boiling water for about a minute before adding the chia seeds and reducing the heat to a simmer for another three to five minutes.
4. Serve with your preferred garnishes!

Notes

1. Black pepper will aid in the absorption of turmeric (curcumin)

42. SLOW-COOKER CHICKEN CASSEROLE

Prep Time:10 Mins

Cook Time:7 Hrs 15 Mins

Servings: 2

Ingredients

- Knob of butter
- ½ tbsp rapeseed or olive oil
- 1 large finely chopped onion
- 1½ tbsp flour
- 650g boneless, skinless chicken thigh fillets
- 3 crushed garlic cloves
- 400g halved baby new potatoes
- 2 sticks diced celery
- 2 diced carrots
- 250g quartered mushrooms
- 15g dried porcini mushroom, steeped in 50ml boiling water
- 2 extremely low salt chicken stock cubes were used to make 500ml of stock.
- 2 tsp Dijon mustard, plus extra to serve
- 2 bay leaves

Instructions

1. In a large frying pan, heat a knob of butter and 1/2 tbsp rapeseed or olive oil, then sauté 1 finely chopped big onion for 8-10 minutes, until softened and beginning to caramelize.
2. Meanwhile, combine 650g boneless, skinless chicken thigh fillets with 1 1/2 tbsp flour, some salt, and pepper in a bowl.
3. Cook the chicken in the skillet with 3 smashed garlic cloves for another 4-5 minutes, or until it begins to brown.
4. Add 400 grams of halved baby new potatoes, two diced celery sticks, two diced carrots, 250 grams of quartered mushrooms, 15 grams of dried and soaked porcini mushrooms with the 50 milliliter soaking liquid, 500 milliliters of chicken stock, two tsp of Dijon mustard, and two bay leaves to your slow cooker.
5. Stir it thoroughly. Cook for 7 hours on low or 4 hours on high.
6. Take off the bay leaves before serving, and add some Dijon mustard to the side.

43. OPEN SMOKED SALMON SANDWICH WITH WHIPPED GOAT'S CHEESE

Prep Time: 10 Mins

Total Time: 10 Mins

Servings: 2

Ingredients

- 4 slices bread of your choice
- 200 g (7 Ounces) smoked salmon
- 100 g (3.5 Ounces) soft goat's cheese
- 2 tbsp sour cream
- 1 tbsp chives finely chopped
- ½ red onion thinly sliced
- 2 tbsp micro greens
- 2 tbsp capers/caper berries.
- fresh lemon juice to taste
- salt and pepper to taste

Instructions

1. Mix the goat cheese, lemon juice, sour cream, salt, and pepper in the food processor bowl. Until smooth, blend.
2. Toast the bread in a hot pan until golden brown for more texture (this step is optional and great to do with day-old bread).
3. Add a generous layer of goat cheese and smoked salmon ribbons to the plate.
4. Add capers, thin red onion slices, and microgreens on the top. Add some freshly squeezed lemon juice and a sprinkle of black pepper to finish.
5. Serve right away.

44. BLUEBERRY PROTEIN PANCAKES

Prep Time: 5 Mins

Cook Time: 15Mins

Total Time: 20 Mins

Servings: 1

Ingredients

- ¼ cup of liquid egg whites
- 1 scoop of vanilla protein powder
- ½ mashed banana
- almond milk if needed
- ¼ cup of fresh or frozen blueberries
- cooking spray
- non-stick pan

Instructions

1. Whisk the egg whites and protein powder in a small bowl using a fork or stir until the protein powder is completely dissolved. A whisk works well for mixing in the protein powder.
2. Add the blueberries and then stir in the mashed banana. You may add a little almond milk to the pancake batter to thin it down if it appears too thick.
3. Set the heat to low-medium and use cooking spray to coat a medium nonstick pan. The key to ensuring that the pancake does not burn is a lower heat setting. Cook until little bubbles appear after adding the pancake batter (about 5 minutes).
4. Make sure the pancake has had enough time to set before you attempt to flip it, otherwise you will wind up with scrambled pancakes instead. Flip the pancake gently to reveal the other side. Cook the pancake until the center is cooked (typically takes another 2-3 minutes). Add your preferred pancake toppings after placing the pancake on a platter. I prefer them with more blueberries and a sprinkle of peanut butter.

45. LENTIL VEGETABLE SOUP

Prep Time: 10 Mins

Cook Time: 35Mins

Total Time: 45 Mins

Servings: 2

Ingredients

- 2 tbsp olive oil
- 1 small finely chopped onion
- 1 finely chopped carrot
- 1 stick finely chopped celery
- 2 crushed garlic clove
- 2 sprigs of fresh rosemary (separated from the stem, then cut finely)
- 3 tbsp tomato paste
- 1 cup of halved cherry tomatoes
- ½ cup of puy lentils
- ¼ tsp chili flakes
- 2 ½ cups of vegetable broth
- 2 slices whole grain bread (cut into 1 cm chunks)
- 5 cups of thinly sliced cavolo nero (alternative mangold)
- 1 pinch of sugar (optional)
- Salt and pepper to taste

Instructions

1. Warm half of the oil in a big pan over medium-high heat, then add onion, carrot, and celery and cook, occasionally stirring, for approximately 8 minutes, until tender and lightly golden brown.
2. Add the garlic, rosemary, and tomato puree and simmer, stirring, for approximately 2 minutes, until fragrant. Cook the tomatoes for 3–4 minutes or until they start to soften slightly.
3. Add the stock, sugar (if using), lentils, and chili flakes. Add salt and pepper, simmer, and then cover with a lid. Cook for about 15 minutes until the lentils are practically soft.
4. Meanwhile, heat the remaining oil over medium-high heat in a skillet. Add the bread chunks and cook for 4-5 minutes, often flipping, until golden brown and crispy.

5. When the lentil mixture and cavolo nero are both done, add the cavolo nero and simmer for an additional 10 minutes. If necessary, taste and adjust the seasoning.
6. After dividing it among bowls, place the croutons on top of the lentil soup.

46. WILD SALMON VEGGIE BOWL

Prep Time: 10 Mins

Total Time: 10 Mins

Servings: 2

Ingredients

- 2 carrots
- 1 large courgette
- 2 cooked, diced beets
- 2 tbsp balsamic vinegar
- 1/3 of a small bag of chopped dill, plus a few more fronts (optional)
- 1 small finely chopped red onion
- 280g poached or canned wild salmon
- 2 tbsp capers in vinegar, rinsed

Instructions

1. Cut the carrots and zucchini into spaghetti-like strands using a julienne peeler or spiralizer, and divide them across two plates.
2. Pour the beetroot mixture over the vegetables after combining it with the balsamic vinegar, chopped dill, and red onion in a small bowl. If desired, sprinkle more dill and capers on top of the flaked salmon.

47. SESAME SOBA NOODLES

Prep Time: 10 Mins

Cook Time: 10 Mins

Total Time: 20 Mins

Servings: 2

Ingredients

Sesame Dressing

- ¼ cup of rice vinegar
- 2 tbsp tamari, more for serving
- ½ tsp toasted sesame oil
- 1 tsp grated ginger
- 1 garlic clove, grated
- ½ tsp maple syrup or honey

For the Soba Noodles

- 6 ounces soba noodles, (see note)
- Sesame oil, for drizzling
- 2 sliced avocados
- Squeezes of lemon
- 2 cups of blanched snap peas
- ¼ cup of edamame
- 2 red radishes or 1 watermelon radish, thinly sliced
- ¼ cup of fresh mint leaves
- Sesame seeds

Instructions

1. Make the dressing: Combine the ginger, garlic, honey, sesame oil, tamari, and vinegar in a small bowl. Place aside.
2. After that, cook the soba noodles according to package directions in a pot of unsalted water. Drain and give a thorough cold water rinse. This aids in removing clump-causing carbohydrates. Divide the noodles into 2-4 bowls after tossing with the dressing. Add the avocado slices to the bowls along with the snap peas, edamame, radish, mint, and sesame seeds after squeezing some fresh lemon juice onto them. If you would like, add extra tamari or sesame oil.

Notes

1. Use gluten-free soba noodles; I prefer these if you can't have gluten.
2. By substituting maple syrup for the honey, you can make this vegan.

48. YUMMY LEMON ZUCCHINI PASTA SAUCE WITH FETA

Prep Time: 5 Mins

Cook Time: 15 Mins

Total Time: 20 Mins

Servings: 1

Ingredients

- 1 tsp Olive Oil
- 1 medium Zucchini
- 2 tsp lemon juice
- 60 g Short Pasta
- 50 g Feta Cheese
- Salt and Cracked Black Pepper to Taste

Instructions

1. Put a sizable pan of water on the stove to come to a boil; after it does, season it and cook your pasta in it as directed on the package.
2. Wash your zucchini, cut off the top and bottom, and chop it into bite-sized pieces. Try to keep the zucchini bite-sized; avoid cutting it into pieces that are larger than the pasta, as you want the lemon zucchini pasta sauce to combine nicely with the pasta.
3. Warm up the olive oil in a frying pan. When it's heated, stir in the zucchini and combine thoroughly.
4. Allow the zucchini to brown on a medium-low heat for 8-10 minutes.
5. Dress the zucchini with half the lemon juice after they are finished cooking.
6. Drain the pasta from the water and return it to the pan with the zucchini once the pasta is done cooking and the zucchini are cooked (they may still have a bit of a bite to them). Add salt, pepper, and lemon juice to dress it.
7. Add the crumbled feta right before serving, combine well, and plate. Enjoy!

Notes

1. The zucchini quantity is indicative; you may use a little more or less depending on taste or supply.
2. You may reheat the zucchini sauce in the microwave or a saucepan. A few tbsp of pasta cooking water should be added to a skillet and mixed well. The pan should then be heated on medium heat until boiling hot before adding the just-cooked pasta.
3. Simply omit the feta cheese and replace it with a vegan version, or top with some grilled peppers, olives, and fresh basil leaves, to make this meal vegan.

49. POACHED EGGS WITH BROCCOLI, TOMATOES & WHOLEMEAL FLATBREAD

Prep Time: 5 Mins

Cook Time: 6 Mins

Total Time: 11 Mins

Servings: 2

Ingredients

- 100g thin-stemmed broccoli, trimmed and halved
- 200g cherry tomatoes on the vine
- 4 medium free-range eggs (fridge cold)
- 2 wholemeal flatbreads
- 2 tsp mixed seeds (such as sesame, linseed, sunflower, and pumpkin)
- 1 tsp olive oil
- good pinch of chilli flakes

Instructions

1. Preheat the kettle. Place an ovenproof plate into the preheated oven at 120°C/100°F/gas 1/2 to warm it up. Bring one-third of a kettle's worth of water to a boil in a large pot. After adding, boil the broccoli for 2 minutes. Return to a boil and simmer for 30 seconds after adding the tomatoes. While you poach the eggs, take them out with tongs or a slotted spoon and lay them on the heating dish in the oven.
2. Bring the water back to a low simmer. Cook for 2 ½ - 3 minutes, or until the whites are set and the yolks are runny, breaking eggs into the pan one by one.

3. Place the tomatoes and broccoli on top of the flatbreads that you have divided across the two plates. Place the eggs on top after draining with a slotted spoon. Add the seeds and the oil, then sprinkle. Serve immediately after seasoning with a little black pepper and the chilli flakes.

50. QUINOA STUFFED EGGPLANT WITH TAHINI SAUCE

Prep Time: 5 Mins

Cook Time: 30 Mins

Total Time: 35 Mins

Servings: 2

Ingredients

- 1 eggplant
- 2 tbsp divided olive oil
- 1 medium shallot diced (about ½ cup)
- 1 cup of chopped button mushrooms about 2 cups of whole
- 5 - 6 Tuttorosso whole plum tomatoes chopped
- 1 tbsp tomato juice from the can
- 2 minced garlic cloves
- ½ cup of cooked quinoa
- ½ tsp ground cumin
- 1 tbsp chopped fresh parsley + more to garnish
- Salt & pepper to taste
- 1 tbsp tahini
- 1 tsp lemon juice
- ½ tsp garlic powder
- Water to thin

Instructions

1. Set the oven's temperature to 425°F. Slice the eggplant lengthwise, then remove portion of the flesh. Put in a baking sheet and cover with a thin layer of oil. Salt the top, then bake for 20 minutes.
2. Warm the remaining oil in a big pan while the eggplant cooks. Add the mushrooms and shallots all at once. About 5 minutes of sautéing the mushrooms should achieve

softness. Cook until the liquid has evaporated before including the tomatoes, quinoa, and seasonings.

3. After that, decrease the oven temperature to 350°F and fill each half of the eggplant with tomato-quinoa mixture after 20 minutes. Bake for another ten minutes.

4. Mix the tahini, lemon juice, garlic, water, and seasonings just before serving. Sprinkle parsley and tahini over the eggplants before eating!

51. VEGGIE POWER BOWL

Prep Time: 20 Mins

Total Time: 20 Mins

Servings: 2

Ingredients

- Two handfuls mixed salad greens
- 1 cup of cooked forbidden black rice
- 1 carrot, peeled into thin ribbons
- ½ sliced avocado
- ⅓ cup of thawed frozen edamame
- ¼ cup of thinly sliced daikon radish
- 1-2 soft-boiled eggs
- Sesame Ginger Dressing, for drizzling
- Sesame seeds, for sprinkling
- 1 chopped scallion, optional
- pickled ginger, optional
- Lemon or lime wedges, for serving, optional
- Sriracha, for serving, optional
- Sea salt and freshly ground black pepper

Instructions

1. Put salad leaves, rice, carrot, avocado, edamame, daikon, and soft-boiled eggs in each bowl.

2. Add the dressing and sesame seeds after drizzling. Add the pickled ginger and, if using, the scallions. Use salt and pepper to taste to season. If preferred, serve with lemon wedges and sriracha.

52. PUTTANESCA PASTA SALAD

Prep Time: 10 Mins

Cook Time: 10 Mins

Total Time: 20 Mins

Servings: 2

Ingredients

- 7 Ounces pasta
- 2 tbsp olive oil
- 1 peeled and halved garlic clove
- 9 Ounces chopped tomatoes, around 2 large tomatoes, seeds removed
- ¼ - ½ tsp dried chilli flakes
- 1 tbsp roughly chopped capers in vinegar
- 12 roughly chopped black olives
- Handful of fresh parsley or basil, roughly chopped/torn

Instructions

1. Cook pasta as directed on the package. Run cooked food under cold water to eliminate starch and chill. (This ought to prevent the spaghetti from sticking together after it cools.)
2. While pasta cooks, heat olive oil and garlic in a small pot. After 3–4 minutes, you'll start to see bubbles around the garlic. Turn off the heat and chill the garlic if you prefer raw garlic.
3. Remove the garlic from the oil and stir in the tomatoes, dried chiles, capers, olives, and parsley or basil.
4. Stir the tomato dressing into the pasta and serve immediately, or store in fridge for a couple of days.

53. GREEK-STYLE ROAST FISH

Prep Time: 10 Mins

Cook Time: 50 Mins

Total Time: 1 Hrs

Servings: 2

Ingredients

- 5 small potatoes, cleaned and sliced into wedges (about 400g).
- 1 halved and sliced onion
- 2 roughly chopped garlic cloves
- ½ tsp dried oregano
- 2 tbsp olive oil
- ½ lemon, cut into wedges
- 2 large tomatoes, cut into wedges
- 2 fresh skinless pollock fillets (about 200g)
- small handful parsley, roughly chopped

Instructions

1. Preheat the oven to 200°Celsius/180°Celsius fan/gas 6. Put the potatoes, onion, garlic, oregano, and olive oil in a roasting pan, season to taste, and then combine everything with your hands to evenly distribute the oil. Roast for 15 minutes, then flip everything over and bake for another 15 minutes.
2. Add the lemon and tomatoes, roast for 10 minutes, then top with the fish fillets and roast for an additional 10 minutes. Serve with a sprinkle of parsley.

54. GRILLED TURKEY-ZUCCHINI BURGERS

Prep Time: 25 Mins

Total Time: 25 Mins

Servings: 2

Ingredients

- 1 medium grated zucchini (1 ½ cups loosely packed)
- 1 pound 85% lean ground turkey
- 1 large egg
- 1 tsp garlic powder
- 1 tsp ground cumin
- ½ tsp kosher salt
- Canola oil, for grilling
- 4 toasted burger buns
- Sliced tomatoes, mayonnaise, Bibb lettuce, honey mustard, and pickles for topping
- Sweet potato chips for serving

Directions

1. Place the zucchini on a clean dish towel, then squeeze out any extra liquid. In a large bowl, combine the squeezed zucchini with the turkey, egg, garlic powder, cumin, and salt. Make 4 equal amounts of the mixture, and then shape each into a 34-inch-thick patty.
2. Heat an oiled grill or a greased grill pan over medium-high heat. Add the patties and cook, turning once, for 5-6 minutes on each side, until a thermometer inserted in the middle of the patties reads 165 F. Serve with chosen toppings and chips on buns.

55. TUNA MELT GRILLED CHEESE SANDWICH

Total Time: 11 Mins

Servings: 2

Ingredients

- 1 can drained white tuna in water
- 1 tbsp mayonnaise
- 1 tbsp chopped green onions
- pinch of salt
- ¼ tsp ground black pepper, or to taste
- 2 tbsp divided unsalted butter
- 4 slices of toast bread
- 4 slices sharp white cheddar cheese
- ½ cup of sharp (yellow) shredded cheddar cheese

Instructions

1. Combine tuna, mayonnaise, and green onions in a small bowl. Place aside.
2. Spread ½ tbsp butter on each of the 4 pieces of bread and arrange them on a dish, butter side down. Equally distribute white cheddar onto 2 of the pieces. Add a thin coating of the tuna mixture and grated cheddar on those same 2 slices. Then place final slice of bread on top of each (butter side on top).
3. Warm a skillet or griddle pan over medium heat. Cook the sandwiches for three minutes on each side, or until golden.

56. COUSCOUS & PEAR SALAD WITH GOAT'S CHEESE

Prep Time: 10 Mins

Cook Time: 12 Mins

Total Time: 12 Mins

Servings: 2

Ingredients

- ½ cup of couscous
- ½ cup of water + 2 tbsp (divided)
- ¼ tsp salt
- 2 handfuls of shredded kale leaves or baby spinach (around 2 Ounces)
- 1 sliced pear
- 3 Ounces diced or crumbled goat cheese
- 1 tbsp maple syrup
- 1 tbsp balsamic vinegar
- ½ tsp olive oil
- Flaky or sea salt

Instructions

1. Optional step: Lightly toast the couscous in a dry skillet for a few minutes, or until it turns a light brown and begins to emit its scent, if you have the time and want. Next, go to step 2. To save time, feel free to altogether omit this step!
2. Add the couscous to a medium salad bowl. Mix in ¼ tsp salt and ½ cup of boiling water before adding a lid and cooking for 8-10 minutes.
3. Sliced pear, goat cheese, baby spinach or broken kale leaves, and add to the salad dish. Pour a good amount of flaky or sea salt on top of the combination of maple syrup, balsamic vinegar, olive oil, 2 tbsp water, and other ingredients. Mix well, then plate.

57. ROAST SEA BASS & VEGETABLE TRAYBAKE

Prep Time: 10 Mins

Cook Time: 30 Mins

Total Time: 40 Mins

Servings: 2

Ingredients

- 300g red-skinned potatoes, finely split into rounds
- 1 red pepper, cut into strips
- 2 tbsp extra virgin olive oil
- 1 rosemary sprig, with leaves cut off and minced very finely.
- 2 sea bass fillets
- 25g pitted black olive, halved
- ½ lemon, sliced thinly into rounds
- handful basil leaves

Instructions

1. Preheat oven to 180°Celsius/160°Celsius fan/gas 4. Place the potato and pepper slices on a large, nonstick baking sheet. Add 1 tbsp of oil, the rosemary, a bit of salt, and plenty of freshly ground pepper. Combine everything thoroughly, roast for 25 minutes, flipping the potatoes over halfway through, or until they are golden and crisp around the edges.
2. Place the fish fillets on top, then sprinkle the olives all around. Add a few lemon slices and the remaining oil to the fish. Roast the fish for a further 7-8 minutes, or until it is fully done. Serve with basil leaves on the side.

58. MANGO GINGER RICE BOWL

Prep Time: 20 Mins

Cook Time: 5 Mins

Total Time: 25 Mins

Servings: 2

Ingredients

- 2 handfuls snap peas, strings removed
- 1-2 cups of cooked short grain white rice
- 1 small carrot, thinly coin-shaped.
- 2 cups of shredded green cabbage
- ½ English cucumber, thinly sliced into coins
- 1 small ripe Ataulfo mango, diced
- ½ cup of cooked drained and rinsed black beans
- 2 tbsp pickled ginger
- ¼ cup of thinly sliced fresh basil
- ¼ cup of toasted peanuts, optional
- Sprinkle of sesame seeds, optional
- ¼ to ½ avocado, optional

Dressing

- 2 tbsp tamari, more for serving
- 2 tbsp rice vinegar
- 2 tbsp lime juice
- 2 garlic cloves, minced
- 2 tsp cane sugar
- ½ tsp sriracha, more for serving

Instructions

1. Make the dressing: Combine the tamari, vinegar, lime juice, garlic, cane sugar, and sriracha in a small bowl.
2. Place a bowl of cold water nearby and bring a small saucepan of salted water to a boil. Place the sugar snap peas in the boiling water for 1½ minutes, then transfer them to the cold water to halt the cooking. Drain, dry off after cooling, and then chop.

3. Put the rice, black beans, pickled ginger, basil, mango, carrot, cucumber, and shredded cabbage in the bowls. Add the avocado, if using, the toasted peanuts, and sesame seeds on top. Pour half of the dressing into bowls and, if preferred, add tamari and sriracha on the side.

59. ORZO, BEAN AND TUNA SALAD

Total Time: 20 Mins

Servings: 2

Ingredients

- ½ finely chopped red onion
- 2 tbsp sherry vinegar
- 150g green beans, cut into bite-sized pieces
- 100g orzo
- 1 tbsp olive oil
- 1 tin drained and flaked tuna
- 3 roasted red peppers from a jar, chopped
- 12 dry-cured black olives, halved
- a handful dill, chopped

Instructions

1. Place the onions, vinegar, and seasoning in a bowl.
2. Cook the beans for 3 minutes in boiling salted water, then remove with a slotted spoon. Cook the orzo in the same water until it is al dente, then drain, rinse under cold water, and drain very well again.
3. Pour the beans, orzo, olive oil, tuna, peppers, olives, dill, and salt and pepper to taste into the dish with the onion. combine, then serve.

60. SMOKED TOFU AND HUMMUS BUDDHA BOWL

Prep Time: 5 Mins

Cook Time: 10 Mins

Total Time: 15 Mins

Servings: 2

Ingredients

- ½ tsp turmeric
- ½ cup of basmati rice (½ cup = 100g)
- 10 Ounces smoked tofu (10 Ounces = roughly 300g)
- 2 tsp olive oil
- 2 handful lamb's lettuce
- 1 small red onion
- 4 tbsp hummus
- 1 tbsp lemon juice
- 6 tbsp water
- ½ tsp salt

Instructions

1. Cook rice according to the package directions. Add salt and turmeric and stir. You are aware that the rice to water ratio is 1:2. Use cold water, bring to a boil, and then cover and simmer for ten minutes. Done
2. Slice the smoked tofu. After that, add some olive oil to a skillet and add the tofu that has been diced. around 7 minutes to fry.
3. Wash the lamb's lettuce and thinly chop the red onion. After that, add both to your bowl.
4. Add the hummus, lemon juice, and water to a small bowl. Mix thoroughly.
5. Time to assemble: fill your dish with the cooked rice and fried tofu. The hummus dressing should now be applied. Add salt, if needed.
6. Enjoy!

61. LIGHTER CHINESE CHILLI BEEF

Prep Time: 15 Mins

Cook Time: 10 Mins

Total Time: 25 Mins

Servings: 2

Ingredients

- 250g lean beef, such as sirloin steak, trimmed of any excess fat
- ½ red pepper
- 4 spring onions, ends trimmed
- 85g Tenderstem broccoli spears
- 100g pak choi (baby pak choi is good)
- 3 tbsp fresh orange juice
- 1 tsp Chinese rice wine vinegar or white wine vinegar
- 2 tsp dark soy sauce
- 1 tsp hot chilli sauce, such as sriracha
- 1 medium egg white
- ½ tsp five-spice powder
- 1 tbsp cornflour
- 1½ tsp self-raising flour
- 1 tbsp plus 1 ½ tsp rapeseed oil
- 2 finely chopped garlic cloves
- 2 tsp finely chopped root ginger
- ¼ tsp chilli flakes, or a good pinch if you prefer it a bit milder

Instructions

1. Place the meat in the freezer 25-30 minutes before cooking. This will slightly harden it up and make it simpler to slice it really thinly.
2. Meanwhile, peel the pepper very thinly after removing the core and seeds. Cut the broccoli spears in half or fourths after cutting through the stems and florets, then slice the spring onions diagonally. Slice the pak choi very thinly. Mix the orange juice, vinegar, soy sauce, and hot sauce together. Place aside.
3. Cut the steak into very thin strips. With a fork, stir the egg white in a bowl until it becomes somewhat foamy. Add the flour, cornstarch, five-spice powder, and meat; swirl until the beef is well covered. A nonstick wok or frying pan should have 1 tbsp of the oil in it. Put the beef in and stir-fry for 3–4 minutes after it's extremely hot

(test by placing a little piece of steak there; it should sizzle quickly). Put aside after being removed using a slotted spoon.

4. After steaming the broccoli spears for 1 1/2 minutes, add the pak choi and continue steaming for an additional 45 seconds to 1 minute, or until both are soft and crisp. To cease cooking and preserve their color, remove and chill under running cold water. Place aside.

5. Then, add the remaining oil and heat the wok once more until it is very hot. Stir-fry the garlic, ginger, red pepper, and spring onions for two to three minutes, or until they begin to turn brown. Add the chilli flakes before adding the soy sauce, orange juice, and water mixture. Stir in the meat and steamed vegetables as it begins to boil, and simmer for a few while to heat thoroughly. Splash in an additional 1-2 tbsp water if you want it to be a bit saucier.

62. CHIPOTLE CHICKEN LUNCH WRAP

Total Time: 35 Mins

Servings: 2

Ingredients

- 2 small chicken breasts
- 2 tbsp chipotle paste
- ¼ shredded red cabbage
- 2 thinly sliced spring onions
- 1 lime, juiced
- 2 handfuls baby spinach
- a large handful coriander, chopped
- 2 large tortilla wraps, wholemeal
- 2 tbsp soured cream
- 2 tbsp chopped pickled jalapeños
- Tabasco, to serve

Instructions

1. Set the oven's temperature to 200°Celsius/180°Celsius/gas. 6. Put the chicken breasts on a non-stick baking sheet, coat with chipotle paste, and season. Place in the oven and bake for 20-25 minutes, or until done. After resting on the tray for five minutes, slice and mix with any remaining juices.

2. Mix the cabbage and spring onions while adding the lime juice and seasoning. After massaging with very clean hands, add the spinach and coriander.
3. Place a tortilla on top of a big sheet of foil on a cutting board, then cover with soured cream. Lay half of the chicken in a horizontal layer on the tortilla, followed by half of the slaw mixture, then, if desired, jalapenos and a dash of Tabasco. Fold each of the tortilla's sides in before using the foil to help you roll the tortilla around itself. Squeeze to encompass the tortilla, then seal the foil. Repeat with the remaining ingredients and tortilla. To serve, cut each in half.

63. SLOW-COOKER CHICKEN CURRY

Prep Time: 10 Mins

Cook Time: 6 Hrs

Total Time: 6 Hrs 10 Mins

Servings: 2

Ingredients

- 1 large roughly chopped onion
- 3 tbsp mild curry paste
- 400g can chopped tomatoes
- 2 tsp vegetable bouillon powder
- 1 tbsp finely chopped ginger
- 1 deseeded and chopped yellow pepper
- 2 skinless chicken legs, fat removed
- 30g pack fresh coriander, leaves chopped
- cooked brown rice, to serve

Instructions

1. Stir well after adding one large onion that has been roughly chopped, three tbsp of mild curry paste, a can of chopped tomatoes that weighs 400 grams, two tsp of vegetable bouillon powder, one tbsp of finely chopped ginger, and one tbsp of yellow pepper to the slow cooker pot.
2. Push 2 skinless chicken legs, fat removed, beneath all the other ingredients until thoroughly immersed. Place the cover on top and refrigerate overnight.
3. Cook the chicken and veggies on Low for 6 hours the following day to make sure they are really soft.
4. Stir in the chopped coriander leaves just before serving over brown rice.

64. KIMCHI BROWN RICE BLISS BOWLS

Prep Time: 10 Mins

Cook Time: 30 Mins

Total Time: 40 Mins

Servings: 2

Ingredients

- 1 cup of cooked brown rice
- Heaping ¼ cup of kimchi (see note)
- 1 Persian cucumber, peeled into ribbons
- ½ cup of thinly sliced red cabbage
- ½ sliced avocado
- 8 ounces baked or grilled Marinated Tempeh
- ½ recipe Peanut Sauce
- ½ tsp sesame seeds
- 2 thinly sliced Thai chiles, optional
- Lime slices, for serving
- Microgreens, for garnish, optional

Instructions

1. Put the rice, kimchi, cabbage, cucumber, avocado, and tempeh in the bowls.
2. Add sesame seeds and Thai chilies, if using, then generously drizzle peanut sauce over top. Slices of lime and the leftover peanut sauce should be served separately. Adding microgreens as a garnish is optional.

65. GRILLED CHICKEN WRAPS

Total Time: 20 Mins

Servings: 2

Ingredients

- 1 (150g) ready-grilled chicken breast, shredded
- 2 wholemeal tortilla wraps
- 20g rocket leaves
- 5 roughly chopped cherry tomatoes

Zhoggiu

- 20g blanched almonds
- 1 roughly chopped garlic clove
- large handful flat-leaf parsley
- large handful of leaves mint
- 1½ tsp white balsamic or sherry vinegar
- 1 lemon, zested to make ½ tsp
- 2 tbsp extra-virgin olive oil

Instructions

1. Toast almonds in a small frying pan over low-to-medium heat for 3 minutes, tossing often, until they are lightly brown. Move right away to a cutting board to cool. Chop roughly before adding the rest zhoggiu components, excluding the olive oil, to a food processor. Pulse till blended but still with some roughness, not entirely smooth.
2. Blend the ingredients together and gradually add the olive oil until the sauce emulsifies. Add 1 to 1½ tbsp of water and blend the sauce if it appears a touch too thick. Scrape into a large bowl, then season as desired. Toss the sauce with the chicken to moisten. Add the shredded chicken. Season.
3. Place the tortilla wraps on a plate, then garnish each with cherry tomatoes and rocket. To wrap each tortilla, divide the chicken mixture between the two. If you won't be eating right away, wrap in foil.

66. GREEN GODDESS CREAM CHEESE VEGGIE SANDWICH

Prep Time: 15 Mins

Cook Time: 6 Mins

Total Time: 21 Mins

Servings: 2

Ingredients

- 1 (7-ounce) container Light cream cheese
- 2 tbsp minced Italian flat leaf parsley
- 2 tbsp minced basil leaves
- 1 tbsp minced tarragon leaves
- 1½ tsp minced chives
- 1 small pressed garlic clove
- ¼ lemon, juiced
- kosher salt and freshly ground black pepper
- 4 slices thick cut sandwich bread
- Extra virgin olive oil
- ½ sliced zucchini
- Fresh baby spinach leaves
- Cucumber, very thinly sliced
- Heirloom green tomato, thickly sliced
- Avocado, pitted and sliced
- Broccoli or alfalfa sprouts

Instructions

1. Mix the parsley, basil, chives, garlic, tarragon, and lemon juice with the cream cheese in a small bowl. Set aside after seasoning with freshly ground black pepper and kosher salt to taste.
2. Preheat a grill pan to high heat. Salt and pepper the zucchini slices after brushing them with olive oil. Then cook for 3 minutes on one side, then flip and continue on the other. Take out of the pan and place somewhere to cool.
3. Spread some of the cream cheese mixture onto one side of each slice of bread.
4. Next, layer the following veggies over the cream cheese mixture on two pieces of bread: slices of zucchini, baby spinach, cucumber, tomato, and avocado. Top with sprouts after adding a dash of kosher salt and additional freshly ground black

pepper. Slice the top piece of bread in half and serve it over the sprouts. Keep any excess cream cheese for another purpose or additional sandwiches.

67. GINGER CHICKEN & GREEN BEAN NOODLES

Prep Time: 10 Mins

Cook Time: 15 Mins

Total Time: 25 Mins

Servings: 2

Ingredients

- ½ tbsp vegetable oil
- 2 sliced skinless chicken breasts
- 200g green beans, trimmed and crosswise halved
- A thumb-sized piece of ginger, peeled and sliced into matchsticks
- 2 sliced garlic cloves
- 1 slice of finely chopped ball stem ginger and 1 tsp of jarred syrup
- 1 tsp cornflour mixed with 1 tbsp of water
- 1 tsp dark soy sauce, plus extra to serve (optional)
- 2 tsp rice vinegar
- 200g cooked egg noodles

Instructions

1. Stir-fry the chicken for 5 minutes in a wok with oil heated over high heat. Add the green beans and stir-fry for an additional 4-5 minutes, or until chicken is just cooked through and the green beans are just beginning to soften.
2. Stir-fry the fresh ginger and garlic for two minutes before adding the stem ginger, syrup, cornstarch mixture, soy sauce, and vinegar. After one minute of stirring, add the noodles. Cook the food until it's all hot and the sauce has coated the noodles. Serve after adding extra soy sauce, if desired.

68. SALMON POKE BOWL

Total Time: 45 Mins

Servings: 2

Ingredients

- 120g rinsed and drained sushi rice
- 2 tsp rice vinegar
- a pinch caster sugar
- a handful sugar snap peas, sliced lengthways
- 1 sliced red pepper
- 1 carrot, peeled into ribbons or shredded
- 2 spring onions, cut at an angle and thinly
- 2 tsp vegetable oil
- 200g skinless salmon fillet, diced into 3cm pieces
- 1 tsp toasted sesame seeds

Dressing

- 1 tbsp soy sauce
- 2 tsp toasted sesame oil
- 1 tbsp sriracha
- 1 lime, juiced

Instructions

1. Cook sushi rice according to the package directions, pour it onto a dish, top with the rice vinegar, sugar, and a pinch of salt. Combine, then allow to totally cool.
2. Add small heaps of sugar snap peas, red pepper, carrots, and spring onions on top of the rice in each of the two bowls.
3. Mix the dressing ingredients in a bowl.
4. Warm a nonstick frying pan until it's hot, then cook the salmon cubes for 1 minute on each side, turning them so they brown all over but are still slightly underdone. Toss after gently spooning into the dressing dish.
5. Place any dressing and the salmon in the bowls, then sprinkle the sesame seeds on top.

69. LENTIL BOWLS WITH AVOCADO, EGGS AND CHOLULA

Prep Time: 5 Mins

Total Time: 5 Mins

Servings: 2

Ingredients

- 1½ cups of cooked lentils
- squeeze of lime
- kosher salt and black pepper (to taste)
- 3 large hard boiled eggs (peeled)
- 2 ounces sliced avocado
- ½ cup of halved grape tomatoes
- chopped cilantro
- few dashes Cholula hot sauce

Instructions

1. Add 3 egg halves, 1 ounce of avocado, 1 tbsp of cilantro, and extra salt and pepper to a bowl with ¾ cup of lentils. After that, squeeze a little lime juice over the top and season with salt and pepper to taste. Add spicy sauce to the end, then indulge!

70. HEALTHY ROAST DINNER

Prep Time: 15 Mins

Cook Time: 50 Mins

Total Time: 1 Hrs 5 Mins

Servings: 2

Ingredients

- 285g thickly sliced medium potatoes
- 4 tiny carrots (160g), cut lengthwise in half
- 2 quartered red onions, each 80g
- 170g large trimmed Brussels sprouts (about 8-10)
- 2½ tsp rapeseed oil
- 2 tsp thyme leaves
- 2 tsp balsamic vinegar
- 1 large finely grated garlic clove
- 2 pinches of English mustard powder
- 170g thick, lean fillet steak
- ½ tsp vegetable bouillon powder

Instructions

1. Preheat oven to 180°C/160°F fan/gas 4. Cook the potatoes for 5 minutes in a big pan of boiling water. Drain and save the water.
2. Toss the sprouts, potatoes, carrots, onions, and 2 tsp of the oil together to coat. Separately arrange on a nonstick baking sheet. Sprinkle with 1 tsp of the thyme, sprinkle with freshly ground black pepper, and roast for 30 minutes.
3. Mix 1 tsp of the vinegar, the garlic, the remaining thyme and oil, the mustard, and a generous amount of black pepper as you wait. Put the steak in a shallow dish, rub this mixture over it, and leave aside. Mix the remaining vinegar with the bouillon, 125ml of the first step's leftover water, and put aside. Roast the vegetables for another 15 minutes after turning them over after 30 minutes.
4. Meanwhile, dissolve butter in a small nonstick frying pan over medium-high heat. Remove the steak from the marinade, brush off the excess, and cook it for 2-3

minutes on each side, or until it is cooked to your preference. Take off to a board and rest there. Pour the remaining marinade into the frying pan and heat until it slightly thickens to create gravy. Slice the steak and serve it with the roast vegetables and gravy on the side.

71. LEMON CHICKEN

Prep Time: 10 Mins

Cook Time: 10 Mins

Total Time: 20 Mins

Servings: 2

Ingredients

- 1 tsp cornflour
- 1 tsp dark soy sauce
- Finely grated zest & juice ½ small lemon
- 2 tsp coconut or canola oil
- 1 skinless chicken breast fillet (about 150g) sliced into 1.5cm slices
- 1 deseeded and sliced capsicum, any colour
- 1 medium trimmed and thinly sliced carrot (around 80g)
- 100g broccoli, cut into small florets
- 150ml chicken stock (made with ½ Massel Plant Based Chicken Stock cube)
- 4 trimmed and thickly sliced spring onions

Instructions

1. Mix the corn flour, soy sauce, and lemon juice in a small bowl.
2. Stir-fry the chicken, capsicum, carrot, and broccoli for 2–3 minutes, or until the chicken is lightly browned and the veggies are beginning to soften, in a large frying pan or wok heated over high heat.
3. Add the chicken stock, spring onions, and lemon-soy mixture to the pan and heat to a boil. Cook for 2 minutes, stirring often, or until the sauce has slightly thickened and the chicken is thoroughly cooked.
4. Serve rice with grated lemon zest on top.

72. ROAST DINNER FOR ONE

Prep Time: 10 Mins

Cook Time: 35 Mins

Total Time: 45 Mins

Servings: 1

Ingredients

- 2 tbsp olive oil
- 1 large chicken breast, skin on
- 2 carrots, cut into rounds
- 6 tiny new potatoes, cut in half (approximately 200g/7 Ounces).
- 1 small onion, cut into wedges
- 3 broccoli spears or florets
- 3 thyme sprigs
- 1 bay leaf
- 150ml warmed chicken stock
- ½ tbsp plain flour

Instructions

1. Preheat oven to 200°Celsius/180°Celsius fan/gas 6. Season the skin of the chicken after applying 1 tbsp of oil. Add the thyme and bay leaf to a small roasting pan together with the potatoes, carrots, onion, and broccoli. Pour the remaining oil over everything, season it thoroughly, and toss to coat. Place the chicken breast on top and roast for 25-30 minutes, or until chicken is done and the vegetables are soft.
2. Take the chicken, potatoes, and broccoli out of the roasting tin and leave them aside while you create the gravy in the roasting pan. Add the stock to the tin and place it over high heat on the stove. Simmer for a few minutes after coming to a boil. Stir regularly to avoid lumps after adding the plain flour. Turn off the heat after the sauce has thickened.
3. Cut the chicken breast at an angle into 3 - 4 pieces. Serve with the potatoes, broccoli, carrots, and onion gravy.

73. CHICKEN AND BROCCOLI

Prep Time: 3 Mins

Cook Time: 9 Mins

Total Time: 12 Mins

Servings: 2

Ingredients

Stir-fry ingredients

- 2 tbsp olive oil, divided
- 2 chicken breasts without bone & skin, cut into bite-sized pieces
- salt and pepper
- 1 batch of Stir-Fry Sauce
- 1 bunch of broccoli, cut into tiny florets with the stems removed
- 1 tsp toasted sesame oil
- toppings: sliced green onions, toasted sesame seeds

Stir-fry sauce ingredients

- ⅔ cup of water
- ⅓ cup of reduced-sodium soy sauce
- 3 tbsp rice vinegar
- 2 tbsp cornstarch
- 2 tbsp honey
- 2 peeled and minced garlic cloves
- 1 tsp ground ginger

Instructions

To make the stir-fry

1. In a big sauté pan, heat 1 tbsp of olive oil on medium-high. Add the chicken breasts and sprinkle with plenty of salt and pepper. Cook the chicken, turning periodically, for approximately 5 minutes or until it is largely cooked through and browned.
2. Make your sauce while the chicken is cooking.
3. Add the remaining olive oil and broccoli after the chicken is browned. Cook the broccoli for 3 minutes or until it turns a brilliant green. Cook for 1 minute more or until the sauce has thickened. Remove from the heat and blend with the sesame oil.

4. Then garnish with green onions and toasted sesame seeds before serving warm. Alternately, transfer to a jar and store in the fridge for up to 3 days.

To make the sauce

5. Stir all ingredients in a small bowl until combined.

74. MAPO TOFU RECIPE

Prep Time: 15 Mins

Cook Time: 10 Mins

Total Time: 25 Mins

Servings: 2

Ingredients

- 2 tbsp vegetable oil
- ¼ pound ground chicken
- 2 finely chopped garlic cloves
- 1 peeled and finely chopped thumb size ginger
- 1 finely chopped jalapeno
- 1 pound drained silken tofu
- 1 tbsp sake
- 2 tbsp soy sauce
- 2 tbsp light soy sauce
- 8 tbsp chicken broth
- 1 tsp tobanjan (Korean chili paste)
- ¼ cup of water
- 8 stalks chopped scallions
- 1 tsp sesame oil
- ½ tbsp of potato starch (mixed with 1 tbsp water)
- salt and pepper to taste

Instructions

1. Add 2 tbsp oil, garlic, ginger, and jalapeño to a large skillet over high heat. Cook for one minute, or until garlic is aromatic. Add the ground chicken and heat for a few minutes, or until the chicken is well cooked. Break up the tofu before adding it and

incorporating it. Add the sake, soy sauce, chicken broth, light soy sauce, and tobanjan, and cook for 2 minutes. Add water after thoroughly combining the scallions. Stir well after adding the potato starch mixture (which gives the texture its sticky quality), then add the sesame oil and season with salt and pepper to taste. Add Japanese rice to the dish.

75. HEARTY ASIAN LETTUCE SALAD

Total Time: 20 Mins

Servings: 2

Ingredients

- 1 cup of ready-to-serve brown rice
- 1 cup of frozen shelled edamame
- 3 cups of spring mix salad greens
- ¼ cup of reduced-fat sesame ginger salad dressing
- 1 medium peeled and sectioned navel orange
- 4 sliced radishes
- 2 tbsp sliced almonds, toasted

Directions

1. Prepare rice and edamame according to package guidelines.
2. Mix the rice, edamame, and salad greens in a big bowl. Add salad dressing and toss to combine. Divide salad mixture between 2 plates and garnish with orange segments, radishes, and almonds.

76. PRAWN & HARISSA SPAGHETTI

Prep Time: 5 Mins

Cook Time: 15 Mins

Total Time: 20 Mins

Servings: 2

Ingredients

- 100g long-stem broccoli, cut into thirds
- 180g dried spaghetti, regular or wholemeal
- 2 tbsp olive oil
- 1 large lightly bashed garlic clove
- 150g halved cherry tomatoes
- 150g raw king prawns
- 1 heaped tbsp rose harissa paste
- 1 lemon, finely zested

Instructions

1. Heat up some water in a pan with a little salt. Boil the broccoli for 1 minute 30 seconds, or until it is soft. Drain, then set apart. After that, cook pasta according to the directions on the package, then drain, saving a ladle of cooking water.
2. In a big frying pan with hot oil, add the garlic clove and cook for two minutes on low heat. With a slotted spoon, remove and throw away, keeping the flavored oil.
3. Add tomatoes to the pan and cook for 5 minutes at a medium heat, or until they start to soften and get juicy. Add the prawns in with a stir, and cook for 2 minutes, or until pink. While stirring, add the harissa and lemon zest.
4. Toss the prawns, harissa, and cooked spaghetti with the pasta water. Add the broccoli in with a stir, then taste and serve.

77. HONEY & MUSTARD CHICKEN THIGHS WITH SPRING VEG

Prep Time: 10 Mins

Cook Time: 40 Mins

Total Time: 50 Mins

Servings: 2

Ingredients

- 1 tbsp honey
- 1 tbsp wholegrain mustard
- 2 crushed garlic cloves
- zest and juice 1 lemon
- 4 chicken thighs, skin on
- 300g unpeeled new potatoes, smaller left whole, larger half
- 1 tbsp olive oil
- 100g spinach
- 100g frozen peas

Instructions

1. Preheat the oven to 200°Celsius/180°Celsius fan/gas 6. Combine the honey, mustard, garlic, lemon zest, and juice in a small bowl. Pour marinade over chicken thighs and season accordingly.
2. Place the fresh potatoes between the skin-side-up chicken and the big baking sheet. Add sea salt after drizzling the oil over the potatoes. Roast the chicken for 35 minutes, or until the skin caramelizes and begins to brown in spots.
3. Add spinach and peas to the roasting pan. Return the dish to the oven for a further 2-3 minutes, or until the spinach has started to wilt and the peas are hot and coated in the mustardy sauce.

78. CAJUN CABBAGE SKILLET

Prep Time: 35 Mins

Total Time: 35 Mins

Servings: 2

Ingredients

- 2 tbsp canola oil
- 8 ounces chicken andouille sausages, sliced diagonally ¼-inch thick (about 1 heaping cup)
- 1 small thinly sliced yellow onion (about 2 scant cups)
- Kosher salt
- ½ small head green cabbage, cored, halved crosswise and sliced ¼-inch thick (about 6 cups)
- ¼ tsp crushed red pepper
- 2 minced garlic cloves
- 3 tbsp apple cider vinegar
- 1 tbsp unsalted butter
- ½ small sweet-tart apple, cored and sliced ⅛-inch thick (about ¾ cup)
- 1 large thinly sliced scallion (about ¼ cup)
- Hot sauce, for serving

Directions

1. Warm a big cast-iron skillet or a high-sided saute pan over medium-high heat. To uniformly coat the pan, add the oil and swirl the pan. Add the sausage slices in a single layer and brown the first side for about 2 minutes. Then cook for 2 minutes on the other side, until browned. Put the sausage pieces in a bowl with a slotted spoon and put aside.
2. Add the onion, a splash of water, and a big pinch of salt to the pan and cook over medium-high heat, scraping up any browned bits. Cook for 5-7 minutes, stirring periodically, until the onion softens and becomes lightly caramelized in areas. Add the cabbage, crushed red pepper, and an additional sprinkle of salt, and simmer, turning regularly, for 6-8 minutes, until the cabbage is crisp-tender. Add another splash of water if the pan ever feels dry.
3. Add the garlic and cider vinegar and cook, stirring regularly, until the majority of the vinegar has absorbed, approximately 1 minute. Returning the sausage to the pan

when the butter has melted and adding the apple, stir periodically for 3-4 minutes, or until the apple slices start to soft.

4. Add the scallion and serve right now with spicy sauce on the side.

79. SWEET & SOUR STIR-FRY

Total Time: 21 Mins

Servings: 2

Ingredients

- 100 g fine rice noodles
- 1 x 227g tin of pineapple chunks in juice
- 2 heaped tspcornflour
- 1 tbsp cider vinegar
- 2 tsp low-salt soy sauce
- 2 tsp sesame seeds
- 30 g cashew nuts
- 4 spring onions
- 2 cloves of garlic
- 2 cm piece of ginger
- 1 fresh red chilli
- 200 g sugarsnap peas
- groundnut oil
- 200 g sprouts , such as alfalfa sprouts, chickpea sprouts, beansprouts
- 1 lime

Directions

1. Cover 100g of fine rice noodles with boiling kettle water in a dish to rehydrate them.
2. Pour the liquid from one 227g can of pineapple chunks into a separate dish, then whisk in 2 heaping tsp of cornstarch, 1 tbsp of cider vinegar, 2 tsp of low-salt soy sauce, and 4 tbsp of water to form the sauce. Set the sauce aside.
3. Preheat a wok or big frying pan over high heat and toast 2 tbsp sesame seeds while it warms up, then transfer to a small bowl.
4. Place the pineapple pieces on the dry pan, then add the 30g of roughly chopped cashew nuts after a minute.
5. Cut 4 spring onions into slices of 2 cm each, then add to the pan. Allow everything to burn and get aggressive while you finely slice 200g of sugar snaps lengthwise, along

with 1 fresh red chilli, 2 cloves of garlic, a 2 cm piece of ginger, and 1 fresh garlic clove.

6. Add the garlic, ginger, and chilli to the pan along with 1 tbsp of groundnut oil. Toss for 30 seconds, then toss for 1 minute with the sugar snaps and the more robust sprouts (200g total). Taste and season to taste after bringing it to a boil for a few seconds to thicken.

7. Serve the stir-fry over drained noodles. Return the empty pan to the fire as soon as possible, add a generous amount of boiling kettle water, and use a wooden spoon to thoroughly scrape up all the yummy sticky deliciousness from the bottom. Stir for 1 minute, until the mixture has slightly thickened, then drizzle it over the stir-fry.

8. Serve with lime wedges for squeezing over any delicate sprouts, like alfalfa, and top with toasted sesame seeds.

80. PASTA WITH SALMON & PEAS

Prep Time:5 Mins

Cook Time:10-12 Mins

Ingredients

- 240g whole-wheat fusilli
- knob of butter
- 1 large finely chopped shallot
- 140g frozen peas
- 2 skinless salmon fillets, cut into chunks
- 140g low-fat crème fraîche
- ½ low-salt vegetable stock cube
- small bunch of chives, snipped

Directions

1. Cook the fusilli per the directions on the package in a pan of boiling water.
2. Meanwhile, soften the shallot by cooking it in a pot with a knob of butter for 5 minutes or until tender.
3. Add the peas, salmon, crème fraîche, and 50ml water. Crumble in the standard cube.
4. Add the chives and some black pepper after cooking for 3–4 minutes or until thoroughly heated through. Toss the pasta in the mixture to coat. Serve dishes.

81. HEALTHY AIR FRYER TURKEY MEATBALLS WITH ZOODLES

Prep Time: 25 Mins

Total Time: 40 Mins

Servings: 2

Ingredients

- ½ pounds zoodles (spiralized zucchini noodles, see Note)
- Kosher salt
- ⅓ cup of plain breadcrumbs
- ¼ cup of whole milk
- 8 ounces ground turkey
- ¼ cup of ricotta
- 2 tbsp chopped fresh parsley
- 1 tbsp finely grated Parmesan, plus more for serving
- ½ tsp dried oregano
- Freshly ground black pepper
- Nonstick cooking spray
- 1¼ cups of jarred tomato sauce

Directions

1. Mix the zoodles with a good pinch of salt in a large bowl. Wait 10 minutes until the zoodles soften and release liquid. Dry them off and put them away.
2. In the meantime, mix the milk and breadcrumbs in a medium dish and let aside for approximately 5 minutes, or until the breadcrumbs soften and absorb most of the liquid. With your hands, combine the breadcrumb mixture with the turkey, ricotta, parsley, Parmesan, oregano, ½ tsp salt, and several grinds of black pepper. Make 12 meatballs that are 1½ tbsp in size and 1 inch in diameter.
3. Set an air fryer at 400 degrees Fahrenheit. Spray cooking spray within the basket, then add the meatballs, allowing some space between them for airflow. About 10 minutes into the air-frying process, flip the meatballs halfway through to ensure even browning on both sides.
4. Meanwhile, cook the tomato sauce over medium heat in a medium saucepan. Decrease the heat to low, stir in the meatballs, and keep warm.
5. Add several grinds of black pepper and ¼ tsp of salt to the zoodles to season. Cook in an air fryer set to 400 degrees Fahrenheit until soft and beginning to brown at the

edges, turning once about halfway through cooking time. This should take around 5-6 minutes. Distribute the zoodles between two dinner plates or shallow bowls, then top with 6 meatballs and drizzle with the heated tomato sauce.

82. SMOKY HAKE, BEANS & GREENS

Prep Time: 15 Mins

Cook Time: 10 Mins

Total Time: 25 Mins

Servings: 2

Ingredients

- Mild olive oil
- ½ x 200g pack raw cooking chorizo
- 1 finely chopped onion
- 260g bag spinach
- 2 x 140g skinless hake fillets
- ½ tsp sweet smoked paprika
- 1 deseeded and shredded red chilli
- 400g can drained cannellini beans
- juice ½ lemon
- 1 tbsp extra virgin olive oil

Directions

1. Preheat the grill to high and put a full kettle of water on to boil. Warm 1 tsp of oil in a large frying pan. Put the chorizo's flesh right in the pan after being squeezed out. Add onion and cook for 5 minutes, breaking up the meat with a spatula until it is brown and covered with juices. Additionally, the onion will be tender and yellow.
2. Put the spinach in a colander and gradually pour the boiling water over it to wilt it before running under the cold water faucet. Using your hands, squeeze out the extra water, then set aside. Place the fish on a baking sheet lined with aluminum foil and rubbed with a little of oil. Add some seasoning, smoked paprika, and a bit extra oil after seasoning.
3. Add the chili to the pan with the sausages and cook for an additional minute before adding the beans, spinach, lemon juice, and extra virgin olive oil. Gently reheat it before adding seasoning to taste.

4. Grill the fish for 5 minutes, or until flaky but not dry; no need to flip. Place a small amount of the bean mixture on each dish, then gently add the fish and any accumulated juices from the tray. Serve.

83. SUN-DRIED TOMATO & ARUGULA LENTIL SALAD

Prep Time: 5 Mins

Cook Time: 25 Mins

Total Time: 30 Mins

Servings: 2

Ingredients

- ½ cup of dry lentils
- 2-3 cups of arugula
- ½ cup of sun-dried tomatoes
- 1 cup of grape tomatoes halved
- 2 tbsp crushed walnuts
- 2 tbsp goat cheese crumbles or vegan cheese crumbles
- 2-4 tbsp Vegan Turmeric Ginger Dressing

Instructions

1. Cook the lentils according per package guidelines.
2. Add sun-dried tomatoes, grape tomatoes cut in half, walnuts, goat cheese, and dressing to the arugula.
3. Enjoy the salads with the cooked lentils added!

Notes

1. Cooked lentils may be frozen for up to three months or kept in the fridge for maximum a week!

84. STIR-FRIED CHICKEN WITH BROCCOLI & BROWN RICE

Prep Time: 10 Mins

Cook Time: 20 Mins

Total Time: 30 Mins

Servings: 2

Ingredients

- 200g trimmed broccoli florets (about 6), halved
- 1 diced chicken breast (approx 180g)
- 15g ginger, cut into shreds
- 2 garlic cloves, cut into shreds
- 1 sliced red onion
- 1 roasted red pepper, cubed, from a jar
- 2 tsp olive oil
- 1 tsp mild chilli powder
- 1 tbsp reduced-salt soy sauce
- 1 tbsp honey
- 250g pack cooked brown rice

Instructions

1. Start a kettle of water to boil and transfer the broccoli to a medium pan that is already heated up and ready to start. Pour the water over the broccoli and cook for 4 minutes.
2. Heat the olive oil in a nonstick pan and stir-fry the ginger, garlic, and onion for 2 minutes. Stir-fry the chicken for 2 more minutes after adding it. Save the water after draining the broccoli. Add the broccoli, soy sauce, honey, red pepper, and 4 tbsp of the broccoli water to a skillet and sauté until cooked through. Serve the stir-fry with the heated rice, following the directions on the package.

85. HEALTHY CHICKEN KATSU CURRY

Prep Time: 20 Mins

Cook Time: 35 Mins

Total Time: 55 Mins

Servings: 2

Ingredients

- 25g flaked almonds
- 1 tsp cold-pressed rapeseed oil
- 2 chicken breasts without bone & skin (about 300g/11Ounces total)
- lime wedges, for squeezing over

For the sauce

- 2 tsp cold-pressed rapeseed oil
- 1 medium roughly chopped onion
- 2 finely chopped garlic cloves
- thumb-sized piece ginger, peeled and finely chopped
- 1 star anise
- 2 tsp medium curry powder
- ¼ tsp ground turmeric
- 1 tbsp plain wholemeal flour

For the rice

- 100g long-grain brown rice
- 2 finely sliced spring onions (include the green part)

For the salad

- 1 medium carrot, scraped with a vegetable peeler into long strips
- ⅓ cucumber, peeled into long strips with a vegetable peeler
- 1 small finely chopped red chilli (deseeded if you don't like it too hot)
- juice ½ lime
- small handful mint leaves
- small handful coriander leaves

Instructions

1. Preheat oven to 220°Celsius/200°Celsius fan/gas 7. Cook the brown rice for 35 minutes, or until extremely soft, in plenty of boiling water.

2. Sprinkle the almonds over a dish after coarsely chopping them in a food processor or using a pestle and mortar. Use a tiny amount of the oil to grease a baking pan. Then coat both sides of the chicken with the remaining oil and season thoroughly. Place the chicken on the tray after covering it with the nuts. Any nuts left on the platter should be pressed onto each breast. Bake for 20 minutes, or until well cooked and browned. Slice thickly after resting on the tray for 4–5 minutes.

3. Make the sauce in the interim. Warm the oil in a medium nonstick pot before adding the onion, garlic, and ginger. Cover loosely and cook for 8 minutes, or until softened and lightly browned, stirring occasionally. Avoid letting the garlic burn by removing the cover for the last two minutes.

4. Add the turmeric, star anise, curry powder, and a generous dash of black pepper. Cook while stirring for a short while longer. Add the flour and well whisk. Add 400ml water to the pan gradually, stirring constantly.

5. Simmer the sauce for 10 minutes, stirring periodically. Cover loosely with a lid if it starts to sputter. Once the sauce is completely smooth, remove the pan from the heat and puree it in a stick blender. To your liking, adjust the seasoning. Stay warm.

6. Add the spring onions and continue cooking the rice for an additional minute. Drain well, then set aside while preparing the salad for a few minutes. Toss the herbs, lime juice, and chillies with the carrot and cucumber.

7. Serve the chicken on two plates with rice, salad, and lime wedges.

86. SPICED CHICKEN WITH RICE & CRISP RED ONIONS

Prep Time: 10 Mins

Cook Time: 25 Mins

Total Time: 35 Mins

Servings: 2

Ingredients

- 2 boneless skinless chicken breasts, about 140g/5 Ounces each
- 1 tbsp sunflower oil
- 2 tsp curry powder
- 1 large thinly sliced red onion
- 100g basmati rice
- 1 cinnamon stick
- pinch saffron
- 1 tbsp raisins
- 85g frozen pea
- 1 tbsp chopped mint and coriander
- 4 rounded tbsp low-fat natural yogurt

Instructions

1. Preheat oven to 190°Celsius/fan 170°Celsius/gas mark 5. Add curry powder after brushing the chicken with 1 tsp of oil. Pour the remaining oil over the onion. Place the chicken and onions in a roasting pan in a single layer. Bake for 25 minutes, or until the meat is cooked and the onions are crisp, stirring halfway through.
2. Rinse the rice and then add it to a pan with the saffron, cinnamon, salt, and 300 ml of water. Put on high heat, give it a quick toss, then add the raisins and cover. Add the peas halfway through and gently simmer the rice for 10-12 minutes, or until it is cooked. Divide the rice between two dishes, then add the chicken and onions on top. Before serving on the side, mix the herbs into the yogurt and season to taste.

87. VEGAN JAMBALAYA

Prep Time: 10 Mins

Cook Time: 35 Mins

Total Time: 45 Mins

Servings: 2

Ingredients

- 2 tbsp olive oil
- 1 large finely chopped onion (180g)
- 4 celery finely chopped sticks
- 1 chopped yellow pepper
- 2 tsp smoked paprika
- ½ tsp chilli flakes
- ½ tsp dried oregano
- 115g brown basmati rice
- 400g can chopped tomatoes
- 2 finely grated garlic cloves
- 400g drained and rinsed butter beans
- 2 tsp vegetable bouillon powder
- large handful of parsley, chopped

Instructions

1. Warm the oil in a large pan over high heat and sauté the onion, celery, and pepper for 5 minutes, stirring occasionally, until softened and starting to color.
2. Stir in the spices and rice, then add the tomatoes and water. Add the beans, bouillon, and garlic and stir. Simmer for 25 minutes, covered, until rice is soft and most liquid is absorbed. In the latter stages of cooking, watch the pan carefully to make sure it doesn't boil dry; if it starts to catch, add a little more water. Add the parsley and serve immediately.

88. CAJUN SPICED SALMON

Prep Time: 20 Mins

Cook Time: 5 Mins

Total Time: 25 Mins

Servings: 2

Ingredients

- 2 salmon fillets, about 140g/5Ounces each
- juice 1 lime
- pinch chilli powder
- ½ tsp ground cumin
- ½ tsp smoked paprika
- ½ tsp ground coriander
- pinch of soft brown sugar
- drizzle of sunflower oil
- steamed rice, to serve

For the salsa

- 1 ripe peeled and diced avocado
- handful cherry tomatoes, quartered
- 2 sliced spring onions
- juice 1 lime
- splash of olive oil
- a bunch of coriander, cut in half and picked into sprigs

Instructions

1. Place salmon in a bowl, add the lime juice, and let the fish "cure" for five minutes. Combine the sugar and all the spices in the meantime. Remove the salmon from the lime juice, then roll it in the spices to coat it fully.
2. Preheat the grill to high. Place the salmon on a greased baking sheet with the flesh-side up. Grill the salmon for 5 minutes, or until it is well cooked and the edges are turning dark. Gently combine the ingredients for the salsa with the coarsely chopped coriander while the salmon is cooking. Serve the cooked fish with the salsa, a side of rice, and some coriander sprigs.

89. THAI PRAWN & GINGER NOODLES

Prep Time: 15 Mins

Cook Time: 15 Mins

Total Time: 30 Mins

Servings: 2

Ingredients

- 100g folded rice noodles (sen lek)
- zest and juice 1 small orange
- 1½-2 tbsp red curry paste
- 1-2 tsp fish sauce
- 2 tsp light brown soft sugar
- 1 tbsp sunflower oil
- 25g scraped and shredded ginger
- 2 large sliced garlic cloves
- 1 deseeded and sliced red pepper,
- 85g sugar snap peas, halved lengthways
- 140g beansprouts
- 175g pack raw king prawns
- handful chopped basil
- handful chopped coriander

Instructions

1. Put the noodles in a bowl and cover them with boiling water. Set aside for 10 minutes of soaking. To prepare a sauce, combine the orange juice and zest with the curry paste, fish sauce, sugar, and 3 tbsp water.
2. Warm the oil in a large wok and add half the ginger and garlic. Cook for one minute while stirring. Stir-fry for three more minutes after adding the pepper. Add the sugar snap peas, toss, and heat for a moment before adding the curry sauce. Add the prawns and beansprouts, and simmer until the prawns just turn pink. After draining, add the noodles, remaining ginger, and herbs to the pan. Serve the noodles after thoroughly mixing the sauce with the noodles.

90. VEGGIE OKONOMIYAKI

Prep Time: 15 Mins

Cook Time: 10 Mins

Total Time: 25 Mins

Servings: 2

Ingredients

- 3 large eggs
- 50g plain flour
- 50ml milk
- 4 trimmed and sliced spring onions
- 1 sliced pak choi
- 200g shredded Savoy cabbage
- 1 red chili, deseeded, and more for serving, coarsely chopped
- ½ tbsp low-salt soy sauce
- ½ tbsp rapeseed oil
- 1 heaped tbsp low-fat mayonnaise
- ½ lime, juiced
- sushi ginger, to serve (optional)
- wasabi, to serve (optional)

Instructions

1. Whisk the eggs, flour, and milk together until smooth. Add the cabbage, pak choi, soy sauce, and half of the spring onions. Pour the batter into a small frying pan with hot oil. Cook for 7-8 minutes, covered, over medium heat. The okonomiyaki should cook for a further 7-8 minutes, or until a skewer put into it comes out clean, after being flipped onto a second frying pan.
2. Place the lime juice and mayonnaise in a small bowl and combine. Place the okonomiyaki on a platter, top with the additional chilli, spring onion, and, if using, sushi ginger, and sprinkle with the lime mayo. Served with wasabi on the side, if desired.

91. MEDITERRANEAN TURKEY-STUFFED PEPPERS

Prep Time: 20 Mins

Cook Time: 30 Mins

Total Time: 50 Mins

Servings: 2

Ingredients

- 2 red peppers (about 220g)
- 1½ tbsp olive oil, plus an extra drizzle
- 240g lean turkey breast mince (under 8% fat)
- ½ small chopped onion
- 1 grated garlic clove
- 1 tsp ground cumin
- 3-4 sliced mushrooms
- 400g can chopped tomatoes
- 1 tbsp tomato purée
- 1 chicken stock cube
- handful fresh oregano leaves
- 60g mozzarella, grated
- 150g green vegetables (spinach, kale, broccoli, mangetout or green beans), to serve

Instructions

1. Preheat oven to gas 5 (190C/170C fan). Remove the seeds, core, and stems from the peppers after cutting them in half lengthwise. Drizzle olive oil over the peppers and season thoroughly. Roast for 15 minutes after placing on a baking sheet.
2. In the meantime, warm 1 tbsp of olive oil in a large pan over medium heat. Stirring to break up the lumps as it cooks, pour the mince onto a platter.
3. Clean your pan, then heat the remaining oil at a medium-high temperature. After cooking the onion, garlic, and mushrooms for another 2-3 minutes, add the cumin.
4. Return the mince to the pan and stir in the tomato purée and chopped tomatoes. Add the stock cube crumbles and simmer for three to four minutes before seasoning with oregano. After removing the peppers from the oven, stuff them as full as you can with the mince. (Don't worry if some slips out; the crispiness will be delicious.) Add the cheese on top, then re-bake for 10 to 15 minutes, or until the cheese begins to turn brown.

5. Serve the peppers carefully on a platter with a mound of your preferred greens that have been blanched, boiled, or steamed.

92. SALMON PESTO TRAYBAKE WITH BABY ROAST POTATOES

Prep Time: 5 Mins

Cook Time: 45 Mins

Total Time: 50 Mins

Servings: 2

Ingredients

- 500g baby new potatoes, cut in half
- 1 tsp olive oil
- 2 large courgettes, cut into small chunks
- 1 red pepper, cut into small chunks
- 1 finely sliced spring onion
- 25g pine nuts
- 3-4 salmon fillets
- juice ½ lemon
- 1½ - 2 tbsp pesto

Instructions

1. Boil the potatoes for ten minutes, or until soft, and then drain. Preheat oven to 200°Celsius/180°Celsius fan/gas 6. Place the potatoes on a baking sheet after tossing them in the oil. Roast for 20 minutes. Place the courgette, pepper, spring onion, and pine nuts in the center of the tray, pushing the potatoes to one side. Place the fish on the other side. Put lemon juice on the veggies and fish fillets (not including the potatoes). Put pepper on everything. Spread pesto over each salmon fillet, then put the baking dish back in the oven for another 12-15 minutes, till everything is well cooked.

93. MUSTARDY SALMON WITH BEETROOT & LENTILS

Prep Time: 10 Mins

Cook Time: 10 Mins

Total Time: 20 Mins

Servings: 2

Ingredients

- 2 tbsp olive oil
- 1 tbsp wholegrain mustard
- ½ tsp honey
- 2 salmon fillets
- 250g pouch of ready-cooked puy lentils
- 250g pack of ready-cooked beetroot, cut into wedges
- 2 tbsp crème fraîche
- 1 small roughly chopped pack dill
- 1-2 tbsp capers
- 12 lemons, zested, and divided into 2 wedges for serving
- 2 tbsp toasted pumpkin seeds
- rocket, to serve (optional)

Instructions

1. Preheat oven to 200°Celsius/180°Celsius fan/gas 6. Combine 1 tbsp of oil, mustard, honey, and some spice. Spread the honey-mustard mixture over the salmon fillets on a baking sheet. Combine the remaining oil with the lentils and beets in a casserole dish, then season to taste. Place both in the oven and cook for 10 minutes or until the salmon is done.
2. Combine the lentils with the crème fraîche, dill, capers, and lemon zest. Serve the salmon with the pumpkin seeds strewn on top, lemon wedges on the side, and, if desired, a rocket salad.

94. TUNA & BUTTERBEAN SALAD

Prep Time: 15 Mins

Total Time: 15 Mins

Servings: 2

Ingredients

- 1 small red onion
- 200g can drained tuna in spring water
- 400g can drained and rinsed butter beans
- 250g pack cherry tomato, halved
- 3 tbsp olive oil
- juice of ½ lemon
- 1 tsp Dijon mustard
- 20g pack roughly chopped flat-leaf parsley

Instructions

1. First, cut the onion in half, then slice it as thinly as you can. Place the tuna in a salad bowl after being tipped in. Add the cherry tomatoes and butterbeans with a gentle toss.
2. Combine the mustard, lemon juice, and olive oil in a bowl, then season. Sprinkle the parsley on top after drizzling the dressing over the salad. Combine gently, then serve right away.

95. HERBY FISH FINGERS WITH CHINESE-STYLE RICE

Prep Time: 10 Mins

Cook Time: 36 Mins

Total Time: 46 Mins

Servings: 2

Ingredients

- 100g brown basmati rice
- 160g frozen peas
- 50g French beans
- 3 finely chopped spring onions,
- ½ tsp dried chilli flakes
- good handful coriander, roughly chopped
- 2 tsp tamari
- few drops sesame oil
- 1 tbsp cold-pressed rapeseed oil
- 2 large eggs
- 280g bag of thick pieces of skinless cod loins (cut into 4 strips per loin)

Instructions

1. Cook the rice for 25 minutes in a pan of water, adding the peas and beans for the last 6 minutes. Drain, then add the spring onions, chilli flakes, everything but 1 tbsp of chopped coriander, tamari, and sesame oil back to the pan. Cover.
2. Meanwhile, heat the rapeseed oil in a big nonstick pan. Combine the eggs and the remaining 1 tbsp coriander. Cut the salmon into chunky slices, then dip in the egg and fry in the oil for a few minutes on each side until brown. After removing the fish from the pan, add the rice and any leftover egg, and mix. Serve in dishes with the fish on top.

96. GINGERY BROCCOLI-FRY WITH CASHEWS

Prep Time: 15 Mins

Cook Time: 10 Mins

Total Time: 25 Mins

Servings: 2

Ingredients

- 320g head of broccoli, split into stalks and florets
- 40g roughly chopped cashews
- 1 tbsp sesame oil
- 15g finely sliced ginger
- 1 small finely chopped red onion
- 1 seeded, and thinly sliced red pepper
- 1 large carrot (160g), cut into thin strips
- 2 thinly sliced garlic cloves
- 1 red deseeded and finely chopped chilli, plus extra sliced, to serve
- 1 tbsp tamari
- 1 lime, juiced and zested
- 7g chopped coriander, plus extra to serve
- 2 eggs, beaten

Instructions

1. Blend the broccoli stalks in a food processor until they are finely chopped. Add the florets and pulse until the texture is rice-like.
2. Place the cashews on a platter and put aside after briefly toasting them in a skillet or frying pan. Add the ginger, onion, pepper, carrot, garlic, and chilli to a pan of hot oil. Stir-fry for 2-3 minutes or until beginning to brown; cover and simmer for an additional 2 minutes.
3. Add the broccoli and 3 tbsp water, and stir-fry for 3 minutes, or until all the vegetables are soft. Add the eggs and stir-fry for a very little period of time to only set the tamari, lime juice and zest, and coriander. Serve with cashews, additional coriander, and extra sliced chili peppers, if desired.

97. CHICKEN & NEW POTATO TRAYBAKE

Prep Time:15 Mins

Cook Time: 1Hrs And 15 Mins

Servings: 2

Ingredients

- 3 tbsp olive oil
- 500g new potatoes
- 140g large pitted green olives
- 1 quartered lemon
- 8 fresh bay leaves
- 6 unpeeled garlic cloves
- 4 large chicken thighs
- bag watercress or salad leaves, to serve

Instructions

1. Heat the oven to 200°C, 180°F, or gas 6. Add the potatoes, olives, lemon juice, bay leaves, and garlic to a large roasting pan after pouring in the olive oil. Toss everything together until it is uniformly covered with oil. Season the chicken thighs, skin-side up.
2. After that, place the roasting pan in the oven and roast for one hour, basting halfway through with pan juices. Check the potatoes and chicken to ensure they are cooked through after one hour, then put the dish back in the oven for a further 15 minutes to crisp the skin.
3. Removing the roasting pan from the oven. Press the roasted garlic cloves with the back of a spoon, remove the skins, and combine the crushed garlic with the beef juices. Serve alongside your preferred salad greens, such as watercress.

98. STEAMED TROUT WITH MINT & DILL DRESSING

Prep Time: 10 Mins

Cook Time: 25 Mins

Total Time: 35 Mins

Servings: 2

Ingredients

- 120g new potatoes, halved
- 170g pack asparagus spears, woody ends trimmed
- 1 1/2 tsp of veggie bouillon powder in 225 milliliters of water
- 80g trimmed fine green beans
- 80g frozen peas
- 2 skinless trout fillets
- 2 slices lemon

For the dressing

- 4 tbsp bio yogurt
- 1 tsp cider vinegar
- ¼ tsp English mustard powder
- 1 tsp finely chopped mint
- 2 tsp chopped dill

Instructions

1. Set a pan of boiling water on to cook the fresh potatoes until they are ready. Cut the asparagus spears in half to shorten them and slice the ends without the tips. Pour the bouillon into a big nonstick skillet. Add the beans and asparagus, cover, and simmer for 5 minutes.
2. Place the fish and lemon slices on top of the peas in the pan. Replace the top and simmer for another 5 minutes, or until the fish flakes easily but is still moist.
3. In the meanwhile, combine the yogurt, vinegar, mustard powder, mint, and dill. Add 2–3 tbsp of the fish's cooking liquid and stir. Serve the vegetables with the fish and herb dressing on top and any lingering pan juices in bowls.

99. VEGETARIAN STIR-FRY WITH BROCCOLI & BROWN RICE

Prep Time: 10 Mins

Cook Time: 20 Mins

Total Time: 30 Mins

Servings: 2

Ingredients

- 200g trimmed broccoli florets (about 6), halved
- 150g vegetarian chopped chicken-style pieces (or similar vegetarian product)
- 15g peeled and shredded ginger
- 2 finely chopped garlic cloves
- 1 sliced red onion
- 1 roasted red pepper, cubed, from a jar
- 2 tsp olive oil
- 1 tsp mild chilli powder
- 1 tbsp reduced-salt soy sauce
- 1 tbsp honey
- 250g pouch microwaveable brown rice

Instructions

1. Put the broccoli into a medium saucepan and cover it with boiling water. Boil for 4 minutes.
2. Heat the olive oil in a nonstick wok and stir-fry the ginger, garlic, and onion for 2 minutes. Add the mild chili powder and stir for a few seconds. Stir-fry the vegetarian chicken-style chunks for an additional two minutes. Save the water after draining the broccoli. Add the broccoli, soy sauce, honey, red pepper, and 4 tbsp of the broccoli water to a skillet and sauté until cooked through. Meanwhile, prepare the rice according to the directions on the package, then serve it with the stir-fry.

100. KEY WEST GRILLED CHICKEN

Prep Time: 5 Mins

Cook Time: 15 Mins

Marinating Time: 4 Hrs

Total Time: 4 Hrs 20 Mins

Serving: 4

Ingredients

- 3 tbsp low sodium soy sauce
- 2 tbsp honey
- 1 tbsp olive oil extra virgin
- 1 lime, zest and juice
- 1½ tsp minced garlic
- 1 tsp Sriracha sauce
- 1 tbsp chopped fresh cilantro
- Small chicken breasts (4)

Instructions

1. **For the marinade:** Combine all ingredients in a small mixing bowl and whisk until the honey is thoroughly combined.
2. Place the raw chicken into a Ziploc bag, then fold the bag's edge down and outward to help keep the bag open.
3. Pour the entire marinade into the bag, then unfold the sides and thoroughly close it, being careful to get rid of as much air as possible.
4. Squeeze the bag lightly to distribute the marinade over each piece of chicken evenly.
5. Place in a small bowl and chill for 2-6 hours.
6. Set the grill to medium-high heat and get ready to cook.
7. Grill the chicken immediately over medium-high heat after removing it from the bag.
8. Turn the chicken over 5-7 minutes later. It should slide off easily. Give it another minute or two if necessary.
9. Cook for 5-7 minutes on the second side or until done.
10. Remove from the grill, and savor!

THE END

Printed in Great Britain
by Amazon